Cambridge Elements

Elements in the History of Philosophy and Theology in the West
edited by
Alexander J. B. Hampton
University of Toronto

C. S. LEWIS ON THE SOUL, GOD, AND CHRISTIANITY

Stewart Goetz
Professor Emeritus, Ursinus College

Shaftesbury Road, Cambridge CB2 8EA, United Kingdom

One Liberty Plaza, 20th Floor, New York, NY 10006, USA

477 Williamstown Road, Port Melbourne, VIC 3207, Australia

314–321, 3rd Floor, Plot 3, Splendor Forum, Jasola District Centre, New Delhi – 110025, India

103 Penang Road, #05–06/07, Visioncrest Commercial, Singapore 238467

Cambridge University Press is part of Cambridge University Press & Assessment, a department of the University of Cambridge.

We share the University's mission to contribute to society through the pursuit of education, learning and research at the highest international levels of excellence.

www.cambridge.org
Information on this title: www.cambridge.org/9781009623308
DOI: 10.1017/9781009623292

© Stewart Goetz 2025

This publication is in copyright. Subject to statutory exception and to the provisions of relevant collective licensing agreements, no reproduction of any part may take place without the written permission of Cambridge University Press & Assessment.

When citing this work, please include a reference to the DOI 10.1017/9781009623292

First published 2025

A catalogue record for this publication is available from the British Library

ISBN 978-1-009-62330-8 Hardback
ISBN 978-1-009-62327-8 Paperback
ISSN 3033-3954 (online)
ISSN 3033-3946 (print)

Cambridge University Press & Assessment has no responsibility for the persistence or accuracy of URLs for external or third-party internet websites referred to in this publication and does not guarantee that any content on such websites is, or will remain, accurate or appropriate.

For EU product safety concerns, contact us at Calle de José Abascal, 56, 1°, 28003 Madrid, Spain, or email eugpsr@cambridge.org

C. S. Lewis on the Soul, God, and Christianity

Elements in the History of Philosophy and Theology in the West

DOI: 10.1017/9781009623292
First published online: May 2025

Stewart Goetz
Professor Emeritus, Ursinus College
Author for correspondence: Stewart Goetz, sgoetz@ursinus.edu

Abstract: C. S. Lewis was an adamant atheist when he entered Oxford University as a student in 1917. By 1931, he was an Oxford don and a Christian. Lewis was someone who did not think highly of climates of opinion, and in his book *The Problem of Pain* he warned against uncritically going along with them: 'I take a very low view of "climates of opinion". In his own subject every man knows that all discoveries are made and all errors corrected by those who ignore the "climate of opinion"'. A climate of opinion exists today that either intentionally or unintentionally disenchants or debunks C. S. Lewis. In this Element, the author explains Lewis's belief in the existence of the soul and how it related to his conviction that happiness consists of experiences of pleasure and is the purpose of life, God exists, and Christianity is true.

Keywords: C. S. Lewis, the argument from reason, the soul, belief that God exists, Christianity

© Stewart Goetz 2025

ISBNs: 9781009623308 (HB), 9781009623278 (PB), 9781009623292 (OC)
ISSNs: 3033-3954 (online), 3033-3946 (print)

Contents

	Introduction	1
1	Reasoning and the Soul	2
2	The Pleasure that Makes Life Worth Living	18
3	Belief that God Exists	30
4	Life's End and Christianity	43
	Bibliography	60

Introduction

Clive Staples (C. S.) Lewis (1898–1963) was an adamant materialist and atheist when he entered Oxford University as a student in 1917. He gradually came to affirm the existence of the human soul in the 1920s, the existence of God in 1929 or 1930, and the truth of Christianity in 1931. In this Element, I explain the philosophical reasons for the changes in Lewis's thought. Though Lewis at times served as an apologist for Christianity, he was first and foremost a philosopher, and it was philosophy that led him to become a theist and a Christian. He wrote, 'I came to believe in God on purely philosophical grounds',[1] and 'I was brought back [to Christianity] ... [b]y Philosophy'.[2] While Lewis taught in the English faculties at Oxford and Cambridge, those who knew him best understood that his first love was philosophy. His brother Warren wrote about Lewis that 'the study of philosophy was to him as inevitable as death will be'.[3] And his close friend J. R. R. Tolkien wrote in his diary that Lewis was 'a scholar, a poet, and a philosopher'.[4]

In the following sections, I focus on Lewis's thoughts about reason, the soul, happiness, God, and Christianity. I acknowledge that my presentation of his views about some of these issues is at odds with the climate of opinion in academia concerning Lewis's thought. However, any serious reader of Lewis should remember that he did not think highly of climates of opinion and warned against uncritically going along with them: 'I take a very low view of "climates of opinion". In his own subject every man knows that all discoveries are made and all errors corrected by those who ignore the "climate of opinion"'.[5]

What constitutes the contemporary climate of opinion that leads to a failure to acknowledge some of the philosophical views of Lewis which I discuss in this Element?

First, under the influence of science and materialism, many members of higher education either deny or misrepresent the apparent nature of reason as '*intellectus* when we "just see" a self-evident truth' and as '*ratio* when we proceed step by step to prove a truth which is not self-evident'.[6] Lewis believed

---

[1] C. S. Lewis, *The Collected Letters of C. S. Lewis: Volume II; Books, Broadcasts, and the War, 1931–1949*, ed. Walter Hooper (HarperSanFrancisco, 2004), 605.
[2] Lewis, *The Collected Letters, Volume II*, 702.
[3] Clyde S. Kilby and Marjorie Mead, eds., *Brothers and Friends: The Diaries of Major Warren Hamilton Lewis* (Harper and Row, 1982), 161.
[4] Quoted in Humphrey Carpenter, *J. R. R. Tolkien: A Biography* (Houghton Mifflin, 2000), 152.
[5] C. S. Lewis, *The Problem of Pain* (HarperSanFrancisco, [1940] 2001), 138.
[6] C. S. Lewis, *The Discarded Image: An Introduction to Medieval and Renaissance Literature* (Cambridge University Press, 1964), 157. See also C. S. Lewis, 'Modern Man and His Categories of Thought', in *Present Concerns: A Compelling Collection of Timely, Journalistic Essays*, ed. Walter Hooper (Harcourt, [1946] in 1986), 65–6.

we are directly aware of and know the nature of *intellectus* and *ratio* from 'the inside', from our direct awareness of them as events occurring in ourselves (in our own minds), which he contrasted with an indirect awareness of them from 'the outside', from our study of the human brain. Against the climate of opinion, Lewis held that 'the inside vision of rational thinking must be truer than the outside vision which sees only movements of the grey matter'.[7]

Second, many people in the academy believe that science has established the non-existence of 'the inside' of a human being as a soul that is distinct and separable from its material body. Contrary to the climate of opinion among the educated in his and our day, Lewis was convinced that the soul exists and he thought that science 'has [not] shown, or, by its nature, could ever show'[8] that the soul does not exist.

Third, many people in the university regularly assume that anyone who believes in the existence of objective value is either a eudaimonist about human well-being or a divine command theorist. Lewis, who believed in the reality of objective value, espoused neither of these positions. Instead, he maintained a hedonistic understanding of happiness, according to which pleasure is intrinsically good and pain is intrinsically evil.

Because Lewis understood that people disagree about the philosophical topics just mentioned after they have thought about them, he believed we should begin philosophically by thinking about the nature of thinking itself. Therefore, I begin Section 1 with what is known as Lewis's 'argument from reason'.

1 Reasoning and the Soul

1.1 From Materialism to Soul-Body Dualism

In a letter from 1930 to his lifelong friend Arthur Greeves, C. S. Lewis wrote that '[c]ertainly ones' [sic] own death [would] be a much pleasanter idea if one [could] be quite rid of the lingering idea that the corpse is alive. I thought I had got over this years ago: but every now and then some old stain of savage materialism starts up and tries to make me believe that it is *me* they will nail in a box and bury'.[9] Lewis had been a materialist and, thus, had believed he was his body. Slowly, but surely, his belief about what he was changed. In a letter to Greeves from October 1916, Lewis was intellectually open to the idea that there is a soul which might be immortal: 'As to the immortality of the soul ...

---

[7] C. S. Lewis, 'Meditation in a Toolshed', in *God in the Dock*, ed. Walter Hooper (Eerdmans, [1945] in 1970), 215.

[8] C. S. Lewis, 'Religion without Dogma?', in *God and the Dock*, ed. Walter Hooper (Eerdmans, [1946] in 1970), 135.

[9] C. S. Lewis, *The Collected Letters of C. S. Lewis: Volume I; Family Letters, 1905–1931*, ed. Walter Hooper (HarperSanFrancisco, 2004), 938.

I neither beleive [sic] nor disbeleive [sic]: I simply don't know anything at all, there is no evidence either way'.[10] By 1918, belief in the reality of the spiritual had become a live possibility. Lewis wrote to Greeves that 'the conviction is gaining ground on me that after all Spirit [a word that in the Idealist tradition of the early twentieth century was used interchangeably with 'God'] does exist... I fancy that there is Something right outside time [and] place, which did not create matter, as the Christians say, but is matter's great enemy'.[11] In 1924, we find Lewis affirming that 'states of mind depend on the states of our bodies',[12] a view which at face value presupposes that the former are ontologically distinct from the latter. In early 1930, Lewis wrote to his friend Owen Barfield that '[t]he "Spirit" or "Real I" is showing an alarming tendency to become much more personal and is taking the offensive, and behaving just like God'.[13]

As I will make clear in Section 1.6, Lewis thought all of us begin with the non-inferential belief that we are souls that are distinct from our material bodies. But he recognized that while many people retain their original belief, others do not. He did not, but subsequently reasoned his way back to his soul-body starting point. A reader of what follows in this and subsequent sections might wonder why Lewis found the issue of what he was so complicated. He well understood this puzzlement. After penning complicated thoughts and arguments about the freedom of the will, petitionary prayer, God's omnipresence and hiddenness, and in anticipation of similar treatments of the soul and body, Lewis wrote that he was

> making very heavy weather of what most believers find a very simple matter... Yes. But it depends [upon] who one is. For those in my position – adult converts [to belief in God and Christianity] from the *intelligentsia* – that simplicity ... can't always be the starting point. One can't just jump back into one's childhood... We have to work back to the simplicity a long way around.[14]

It was a long way around for Lewis to get back to the point where he could write in answer to the question What is a soul? 'I am. (This is the only possible answer: or expanded, "A soul is that which can say I am")'.[15] In Sections 1.2

---

[10] Lewis, *The Collected Letters, Volume I*, 235.
[11] Lewis, *The Collected Letters, Volume I*, 374.
[12] Lewis, *The Collected Letters, Volume I*, 621.
[13] Lewis, *The Collected Letters, Volume I*, 882–3.
[14] C. S. Lewis, *Letters to Malcolm: Chiefly on Prayer* (Harcourt, [1964] 1992), 77–8. Elizabeth Anscombe, whose criticism of Lewis's *argument from reason* I will discuss later in this section, wrote to her friend Iris Murdoch, that '[n]o *second rate* philosophy is any good ... One must start from scratch – [and] it takes a very long time to reach scratch'. Clare Mac Cumhaill and Rachel Wiseman, *Metaphysical Animals: How Four Women Brought Philosophy Back to Life* (Chatto & Windus, 2022), 188.
[15] C. S. Lewis, *The Collected Letters of C. S. Lewis: Volume III; Narnia, Cambridge, and Joy, 1950–1963*, ed. Walter Hooper (HarperSanFrancisco, 2007), 10.

through 1.6, I present the intellectual journey that led him back from materialism to a belief in the existence of the soul.

1.2 The Argument from Reason

About his friend Owen Barfield, Lewis wrote

> he convinced me [as part of a protracted philosophical dispute between, roughly, 1923 and 1928] that the positions we had hitherto held left no room for any satisfactory theory of knowledge. We had been ... 'realists'; that is, we accepted as rock-bottom reality the universe revealed by the senses. But at the same time we continued to make for certain phenomena of consciousness all the claims that really went with a theistic or idealistic view. We maintained that abstract thought (if obedient to logical rules) gave indisputable truth ... The view [realism] was, I think, common at the time; it runs through ... Lord [Bertrand] Russell's 'Worship of a Free Man'. Barfield convinced me that it was inconsistent... I was therefore compelled to give up realism.[16]

It is not obvious what Lewis meant when he said that Barfield and he had maintained that abstract thought that obeys logical rules yields indisputable truth and is inconsistent with realism. However, his point about abstract thought obeying logical rules seems to foreshadow his development of what is now known as his 'argument from reason' in which the central point is roughly that causation of one thought by another that obeys logical rules is an immaterial, supernatural sequence of events that occurs in a soul.

To understand Lewis's argument from reason, we must first consider what Lewis had to say about thought as *mental* in nature. Lewis wrote, '[my] thoughts [are] directly present to me',[17] and '[i]t seemed to me self-evident that one essential property of love, hate, fear, hope, or desire was attention to their object. To cease thinking *about* ... the woman is, so far, to cease loving; to cease thinking *about* ... the dreaded thing is, so far, to cease being afraid'.[18] Lewis regarded the *aboutness* or *intentionality* of thinking (thought) as essential to it: 'Acts of thinking are ... a very special sort of events. They are "about" something [typically, but not necessarily] other than themselves and can be true or false'.[19] In Lewis's examples, one thought is about a particular woman and another about a dreaded thing. To think about a woman is to think *that* she is a certain way. For example, it is to think that she is married, that she is the mother of children, that she is the owner of a car, and so on. To think about a dreaded thing is to think that it is menacing, that it is capable of inflicting harm,

---

[16] C. S. Lewis, *Surprised by Joy: The Shape of My Early Life* (Harcourt, 1955), 208–9.
[17] Lewis, *The Problem of Pain*, 21.   [18] Lewis, *Surprised by Joy*, 218. The emphases are mine.
[19] C. S. Lewis, *Miracles: A Preliminary Study*, 2nd ed. (HarperSanFrancisco, [1960] 2001), 25.

and so on. Philosophers standardly refer to thinking as a *propositional attitude*, where a propositional attitude is an attitude of mind like thought, belief, desire, and hate that is directed at a proposition or statement with its *content* or meaning (the phrase following the word 'that': she is married, she is the mother of children, she is the owner of a car) which represents the world as being a certain way (a woman being married, having children, owing a car). In the quote at the outset of this paragraph, Lewis also mentioned love, hate, fear, hope, and desire. He understood that you might not only think that the woman is married but also love that she is married, hate that she is married, fear that she is married, hope that she is married, and so on. Thus, love, hate, fear, hope, and desire are also propositional attitudes. Finally, the content at which a propositional attitude is directed is what makes the attitude mental in nature. A *mind* is that thing which can have propositional attitudes with their contents. Propositional attitudes with their contents make clear that 'our minds must divide and pigeon-hole'.[20]

Barfield argued, and Lewis was convinced, that they had to abandon philosophical 'realism'. In an entry from 1923 in his diary, Lewis wrote of Barfield that '[h]e has completely lost his materialism',[21] and he did so because of 'the nature of thought'.[22] As materialists, they had, as I have already quoted at the outset of this section, 'maintained that abstract thought (if obedient to logical rules) gave indisputable truth'. What did Lewis (and Barfield) believe about causally related sequential thoughts that, when they obey logical rules, is inconsistent with materialism? Lewis provided his most detailed answer to this question in his book *Miracles*, which was published in 1948, and in an assortment of short essays. In these written works, he set out his *argument from reason* against the backdrop of the philosophical view known as *naturalism*.

What is naturalism? Lewis regarded it as the philosophical view that our world is a causally interlocked system of material events. That is, any and every material event that occurs in our world is in principle completely causally explicable in terms of other material events (for the sake of discussion, it is assumed that there are no uncaused or causally indeterministic occurrences like quantum events). There is never the need to go outside the material world and its causal events to explain a material effect event. The material world is *causally closed* to (it in principle excludes) any causal explanation of a material event that is not another material event.

---

[20] C. S. Lewis, *The Four Loves* (Harcourt, [1960] 1988), 128.
[21] C. S. Lewis, *All My Road before Me: The Diary of C. S. Lewis*, ed. Walter Hooper (Harcourt, 1991), 278.
[22] Lewis, *All My Road before Me*, 278.

To ward off the suggestion that Lewis was setting up and knocking down a straw man, which is an objection Lewis himself faced ('Dr [W. Norman] Pittenger thinks the Naturalist whom I try to refute ... is a man of straw... He is quite common where I come from ...'[23]), consider what more recent naturalists say about a mental explanation of a material event. I begin with the following comments from the philosopher Alex Rosenberg:

> Our conscious thoughts are very crude indicators of what is going on in our brain. We fool ourselves into treating these conscious markers as thoughts about what we want and about how to achieve it, about plans and purposes. We are even tricked into thinking they somehow bring about behavior. We are mistaken about all of these things... You cannot treat the interpretation of behavior in terms of purposes and meaning as conveying real understanding... [T]he individual acts of human beings [are] unguided by purpose ... What individuals do, alone or together, over a moment or a month or a lifetime, is really just the product of the process of blind variation and environmental filtration operating on neural circuits in their heads.[24]

According to Rosenberg, a real (correct) understanding of our behaviour must be in the form of explanations that do not include what is mental in nature. The naturalist Richard Rorty agrees, and he provides the following concise summary of the implications of naturalism for explaining events in our world:

> Every speech, thought, theory, poem, composition and philosophy will turn out to be completely predictable in purely naturalistic terms. Some atoms-and-the-void account of micro-processes within individual human beings will permit the prediction of every sound or inscription which will ever be uttered.[25]

Finally, the naturalist Georges Rey has this to say about an explanation for a supposedly mental event:

> Any ultimate explanation of mental phenomena will have to be in *non*-mental terms, or else it won't be an *explanation* of it. There might be an explanation of some mental phenomena in terms of others – perhaps *hope* in terms of *belief* and *desire* – but if we are to provide an explanation of all mental phenomena, we would in turn have to explain such mentalistic explainers until finally we reached entirely non-mental terms.[26]

---

[23] C. S. Lewis, 'Rejoinder to Dr Pittenger', in *God in the Dock*, ed. Walter Hooper (Harcourt, [1958] in 1970), 179.

[24] Alex Rosenberg, *The Atheist's Guide to Reality: Enjoying Life without Illusions* (W. W. Norton, 2011), 210, 213, 244, 255.

[25] Richard Rorty, *Philosophy and the Mirror of Nature* (Princeton University Press, 1979), 387.

[26] Georges Rey, *Contemporary Philosophy of Mind* (Blackwell, 1997), 21.

Lewis came to believe that an implication of naturalism is that it excludes reasoning, 'the connecting by inference of propositions',[27] which is obedient to logical rules. That is, naturalism makes it impossible to infer a conclusion that follows validly from a set of premises. An example is likely helpful at this point. Consider the following instance of reasoning which Bertrand Russell might have followed in preparation for writing the essay to which Lewis referred in the quote at the outset of this section:

1. If man is the result of natural causes (e.g., the accidental collocation of atoms) which had no prevision for the effect they were producing, then ultimately the world of nature cares nothing about the fulfilment of man's deepest desire for perfect happiness.
2. Man is the result of natural causes which had no prevision for the effect they were producing.

Therefore,

3. Ultimately, the world of nature cares nothing about the fulfilment of man's deepest desire for perfect happiness.[28]

Lewis understood that naturalism, which implies that the mental events involved in reasoning must in principle be completely explicable in non-mental terms, 'is really a theory that there is no reasoning'.[29] If naturalism is true, then 'what we thought to be our inferences'[30] are not inferences. Lewis explained his point as follows: When we reason, we are passive. We are patients. What this means is that when we understand, are aware of, apprehend, see, or grasp (Lewis used the terms interchangeably) premises 1 and 2, we *cannot help* inferring and understanding the conclusion 3. We cannot help inferring 3 because we are *causally determined* to infer it. One *event* of apprehension causes another *event* of apprehension. Lewis wrote that '[o]ne thought can cause another not by *being*, but by being *seen to be*, a ground for it'.[31] 'I am quite convinced that my acts [events] of thought ... are not free but determined. E.g. if the truths A > B and B > C are both present to my mind I *must* think A > C. I have no choice'.[32]

> Hence acts of inference can, and must, be considered in two different lights. On the one hand they are subjective events, items in somebody's

---

[27] C. S. Lewis, *The Abolition of Man* (HarperSanFrancisco, [1944] 2001), 31.
[28] Bertrand Russell, 'A Free Man's Worship', in *The Meaning of Life*, 2nd ed., ed. E. D. Klemke (Oxford University Press, [1957] in 2000), 71–7.
[29] Lewis, *Miracles*, 27.   [30] Lewis, *Miracles*, 32.   [31] Lewis, *Miracles*, 25.
[32] Lewis, *The Collected Letters, Volume III*, 1351. Lewis believed all causes determine/necessitate their effects, though he understood that '[s]ome modern scientists seem to think ... the

psychological history. On the other hand, they are insights into, or knowings of, something other than themselves. What from the first point of view is the psychological transition from thought A to thought B, at some particular moment in some particular mind, is, from the thinker's point of view a perception of an implication (if A, then B). When we are adopting the psychological point of view we may use the past tense. 'B *followed* A in my thoughts'. But when we assert the implication we always use the present – B *follows* from A'.[33]

In sum, when we reason there is mental-to-mental causation in the mode of one event of apprehension of content causally determining another event of apprehension of content, and we know from 'the inside' (see the Introduction) that what is mental in nature and the causation involving it cannot be reduced to or eliminated in favour of an instance of material-to-material causation. But such a reduction or elimination is precisely what naturalism demands:

> Any thing which professes to explain our reasoning fully without introducing an act of knowing thus solely determined by what is known, is really a theory that there is no reasoning.
> But this, it seems to me, is what Naturalism is bound to do. It offers what professes to be a full account of our mental behaviour; but this account, on inspection, leaves no room for the acts of knowing or insight on which the whole value of our thinking, as a means to truth, depends.[34]

As a response to Lewis's argument, a person might try to find a semi-real status for thought and reasoning. For example, he might admit the apprehension of content is genuinely mental (it has aboutness) but hold that every occurrence of it is completely causally determined by material events. Lewis responded that if this were the case, then thought would be the 'irrelevant product of cerebral motions'.[35] Lewis cited the following words from J. B. S. Haldane to illustrate his point: 'If my mental processes are determined wholly by the motions of atoms in my brain, I have no reason to suppose that my beliefs are true ... and hence I have no reason for supposing my brain to be composed of atoms'.[36] In other words, to suppose that thought involved in reasoning is really about something but nevertheless completely explicable in terms of material causes would imply that there is no reasoning to a belief, even if the belief happened to be true.

---

individual unit of matter ... moves in an indeterminate ... fashion.... Those who like myself have had a philosophical ... education find it almost impossible to believe that the scientists really mean what they seem to be saying'. *Miracles*, 18, 20.

[33] Lewis, *Miracles*, 26.   [34] Lewis, *Miracles*, 27.
[35] C. S. Lewis, 'Evil and God', in *God in the Dock*, ed. Walter Hooper (Eerdmans, [1941] in 1970), 21.
[36] Lewis, *Miracles*, 22.

Lewis's argument from reason can itself reasonably be understood as reducing to absurdity the assumption of the truth of naturalism:

> I remember once being shown a certain kind of knot which was such that if you added one extra complication to make assurance doubly sure you suddenly found that the whole thing had come undone in your hands and you had only a bit of string. It is like that with naturalism. It goes on claiming territory after territory: first the inorganic, then the lower organisms, then man's body, then his emotions. But when it takes the final step and we attempt a naturalistic account of thought itself, suddenly the whole thing unravels. The last fatal step has invalidated all the preceding ones: for they were all reasonings and reason itself has been discredited.[37]
>
> But you cannot go on 'explaining away' for ever: you will find that you have explained explanation [inferential reasoning] itself away.[38]

Against the background of naturalism, Lewis concluded that reasoning is philosophically correctly regarded as, though it sounds odd to the ear, a *supernatural* occurrence. This is because in reasoning

> the human mind ... is set free, in the measure required, from the huge nexus of non-rational causation; free from this to be [causally] determined by the truth known...
>
> To call the act of [inference] ... 'supernatural', is some violence to our ordinary linguistic usage. But of course we do not mean by this that it is spooky, or sensational, or even (in any religious sense) 'spiritual'. We mean only that it 'won't fit in'; that such an act, to be what it claims to be ... cannot be merely the exhibition at a particular place and time of that total, and largely mindless, system of events called 'Nature'. It must break sufficiently free from that universal [causal] chain to be [causally] determined by what it knows.[39]

It is important to make clear that Lewis's argument from reason was not an argument for the conclusion that we never reason incorrectly. There can be occasions where mental causes do not logically justify the mental apprehensions of conclusions which they produce. For example, a person's desire to believe that an author wrote something can produce the belief that he did, when a careful reading of a text makes clear that the belief is false. Lewis pointed out that it is the existence of cases wherein the mental causes do not justify the

---

[37] Lewis, 'Religion without Dogma', 137–8.
[38] Lewis, *The Abolition of Man*, 81. Though Lewis devoted little space to the Christian theological doctrine of total depravity, he thought it was as indefensible as naturalism: 'I disbelieve [the doctrine of Total Depravity], partly on the logical ground that if our depravity were total we should not know ourselves to be depraved', (Lewis, *The Problem of Pain*, 61). Lewis believed a proponent of total depravity could preach at, but not argue with you, because to do the latter requires that your reasoning not be depraved.
[39] Lewis, *Miracles*, 34–5.

mental effects that leads to the practice of trying to discredit what someone thinks by asserting that what is thought is caused: 'To be caused is not to be proved... The mere existence of causes for a belief is popularly treated as raising a presumption that it is groundless, and the most popular way of discrediting a person's opinions is to explain them causally – "You say that *because* (Cause and Effect) you are a capitalist, or a hypochondriac, or a mere man, or only a woman"'.[40] In lengthier inferences, misremembering what came before can cause the reaching of a wrong conclusion. 'It should ... be remembered that human reasoners often make mistakes ... by inadvertence in the argument itself'.[41] And the attention and apprehension of contents that are required for reasoning might be interrupted by toothache, anxiety, or the stupor from alcohol and never be completed. These events are 'interfering with your consciousness: but not to produce some new variety of reasoning, only ... to suspend [reasoning] altogether'.[42] Lewis's point about the nature of reasoning was that *if* you successfully attend to and apprehend A > B and B > C, then, provided there is no interference, you will be causally determined by that apprehension to apprehend A > C.

Finally, Lewis believed that if you grasp the truth that A > B and B > C implies A > C, and see the falsehood of A > B and C > A implies A > C, then you are apprehending the 'wholly immaterial relation which we call truth or falsehood'.[43]

1.3 Two Critics

Not surprisingly, Lewis's argument from reason has had its critics. Consider two. First, Elizabeth Anscombe questioned Lewis's reasoning in a paper she read at a meeting with Lewis in attendance. She argued that

> on [the naturalistic] hypothesis there would be no difference between the conclusions of the finest scientific reasoning and the thoughts a man has because a bit of bone is pressing on his brain. In one way, this is true. Suppose that the kind of account which the 'naturalist' imagines, were actually given in the two cases. We should have two accounts [explanations] of processes in the human organism. 'Valid', 'true', 'false' would not come into either of the accounts. That shows, you say, that the conclusions of the scientist would be just as irrational as those of the other man. But that does not follow at

---

[40] Lewis, *Miracles*, 24. Lewis termed this popular way of discrediting belief, 'Bulverism' ('Bulverism', in *God in the Dock*, ed. Walter Hooper (Eerdmans, [1944] in 1970), 271–7). He regarded Bulverism as 'a truly democratic game in the sense that all can play it all day long' (Lewis, 'Bulverism', 273). 'Each side can go on playing *ad nauseum*, but when all the mud has been flung every man's views still remain to be considered on their merits'. (C. S. Lewis, 'A Reply to Professor Haldane', in *On Stories and Other Essays on Literature*, ed. Walter Hooper (Harcourt Brace, [1966] in 1982), 75.
[41] Lewis, *The Problem of Pain*, 19.   [42] See Lewis, *Miracles*, 39.
[43] Lewis, 'Religion without Dogma', 136.

all. Whether his conclusions are rational or irrational is settled by considering the chain of reasoning that he gives and whether his conclusions follow from it. When we are giving a causal account of this thought, e.g. an account of the physiological processes which issue in the utterance of his reasoning, we are not considering his utterances from the point of view of evidence, reasoning, valid argument, truth, at all; we are considering them merely as events. Just *because* that is how we are considering them, our description has in itself no bearing on the question of 'valid', 'invalid', 'rational', 'irrational', and so on.[44]

Anscombe made two distinctions in her argument. First, she pointed out the non-temporal nature of valid and invalid logical relations between propositions. For example, 'if P then Q', 'P', therefore 'Q' expresses a non-temporal valid logical relation, while 'if P then Q', 'Q', therefore 'P' expresses a non-temporal invalid logical relation. Second, she made clear the difference between what she regarded as the temporal *physical* causal relations between events in reasoning and the non-temporal valid logical relations tracked or followed by that reasoning. That is, she maintained there is a temporal physical causal relationship that occurs between an awareness of both 'if P then Q', and 'P', and an awareness of 'Q' that tracks or maps the non-temporal valid logical relationship that exists between 'if P then Q', 'P', and 'Q'.

Lewis believed Anscombe made some important distinctions in her paper, and he rewrote Chapter 3 of *Miracles* to take into consideration some of the points she had made. Nevertheless, he continued to maintain that his argument from reason was sound. Most importantly, he believed that Anscombe's critique of his argument assumed a position on the very question at issue, which was whether or not all causation is physical in nature. Lewis believed Anscombe simply took for granted that when one is giving a causal account of the relationship between events of awareness in a process of reasoning, one is giving an account in terms of physical processes. But he insisted that this is what is being disputed. While Lewis agreed with Anscombe that reasoning involves causation, he continued to maintain that because the causation in reasoning is between events of awareness, it is not physical but mental in nature. He insisted that what naturalism in principle excludes is not causation *per se* but mental causation.

Peter van Inwagen is a second critic of Lewis's argument from reason. According to van Inwagen, in Lewis's view a cause-effect 'because'

---

[44] Elizabeth Anscombe, 'A Reply to Mr. C. S. Lewis's Argument that "Naturalism" Is Self-Refuting', in *The Collected Philosophical Papers of G. E. M. Anscombe: Volume 2, Metaphysics and the Philosophy of Mind* (University of Minnesota Press, [circa 1947] in 1981), 226–7.

explanation of a belief fact (an example of a belief fact is a belief that C. S. Lewis was a Cambridge professor) implies that the proposition 'C. S. Lewis was a Cambridge professor', which is the content of the belief, is not accepted rationally by its subject simply in virtue of the belief being an effect event in a cause-effect 'because' explanation.[45]

Van Inwagen assumes Lewis held that the mere fact that a belief is caused excludes the possibility of that belief's being accepted rationally. But this was not Lewis's view. Lewis believed the problem created by naturalism for reasoning was not that a belief fact has a cause but that the truth of naturalism excludes a certain kind of cause of the belief fact, namely, a mental cause.

Van Inwagen also writes in his criticism of Lewis's argument from reason that '[i]f a human being ... can have beliefs, there seems to be no reason to deny that that human being's believing certain things might be the *cause* of his or her believing certain other things'.[46] Lewis would have agreed with this statement, but would have insisted that believing a proposition involves an apprehension of content, and an apprehension of content is a mental event. Van Inwagen also asserts that Lewis failed to show that a belief fact cannot be fully explained naturalistically in terms of the way the universe was in the past and the laws of physics.[47] In response, Lewis would likely have queried whether mental apprehensions are part of the explanatory apparatus of the laws of physics. Do we find physicists describing the world in terms of apprehensions (seeings, graspings, understandings, etc)? If not (as seems to be the case with any traditional physics), then Lewis would have responded that a full explanation of a belief fact in terms of the way the universe was in the past and the laws of physics would ensure that the belief fact was not a causal result of reasoning. However, if naturalism is compatible with a 'physics' that includes mental explanations, then Lewis would have answered that he was not attacking this version of naturalism.

Lewis argued that naturalism undermines reasoning. It is important to understand that naturalism remains to this day the dominant philosophical view in universities and colleges in the western world. For example, the philosopher Timothy Williamson writes that 'many contemporary philosophers describe themselves as naturalists'.[48] Another philosopher, Barry Stroud, states that '"Naturalism" seems to me ... rather like "World Peace." Almost everyone swears allegiance to it, and is willing to march under its banner'.[49] And van

---

[45] Peter van Inwagen, 'C. S. Lewis' Argument against Naturalism', *Journal of Inklings Studies* 1 (2011): 35.
[46] Van Inwagen, 'C. S. Lewis' Argument against Naturalism', 36.
[47] Van Inwagen, 'C. S. Lewis' Argument against Naturalism', 34–8.
[48] Timothy Williamson, 'What Is Naturalism?', *The New York Times*, 4 September 2011.
[49] Barry Stroud, 'The Charm of Naturalism', in *Naturalism in Question*, ed. Mario De Caro and David Macarthur (Harvard University Press, 2004), 22.

Inwagen acknowledges that 'Naturalism was a popular doctrine (popular among scientifically-minded philosophers and philosophically-minded scientists) in the 1940s when Lewis devised his argument against it, and it is if anything even more popular today'.[50] Therefore, Lewis's argument from reason is as relevant today as it was when he first developed it.

1.4 We Must Begin with Reasoning

Lewis believed that proponents of naturalism seldom, if ever, start out believing in the truth of naturalism. Rather, they typically affirm naturalism on the basis of reasoning from the nature of scientific experiments to the conclusion that nature is a causally closed interlocking system:

> Naturalism is a prime specimen of that towering speculation, discovered from practice and going far beyond experience ... Nature is not an object that can be presented either to the senses or the imagination. It can be reached only by the most remote inferences... It is the hoped for, the assumed, unification in a single interlocked system of all the things inferred from our scientific experiments.[51]

Like Lewis, the naturalist Alex Rosenberg believes naturalism looks to science for its justification: 'Naturalism is the philosophical theory that treats science as our most reliable source of knowledge'.[52] An examination of the naturalist's attempt to justify inferentially a belief in naturalism from the nature of scientific experimentation is beyond the scope of this Element.[53] What is important to recognize for present purposes is simply that Lewis believed naturalists typically, if not always, arrive at their belief in naturalism on the basis of inferences that their philosophical theory, if true, makes impossible. He maintained that one can argue against reasoning only by using reasoning. Similarly, one needs to use reasoning to support reasoning. He concluded that '[r]eason is our starting point. There can be no question either of attacking or defending it'.[54]

1.5 Belief in the Existence of the Soul

According to Lewis, our reasoning is supernatural in nature in the sense that it is explained in terms of mental causation that cannot occur in a naturalistic framework. But why maintain, as Lewis did, that this supernatural reasoning occurs in a thing or substance that we denote with 'I' ('Every train of thought is accompanied by what Kant called "the *I think*"'.[55]) And why think that this *I* is a soul?

---

[50] Van Inwagen, 'C. S. Lewis' Argument against Naturalism', 28. [51] Lewis, *Miracles*, 33–4.
[52] Alex Rosenberg, 'Why I Am a Naturalist', *The New York Times*, 17 September 2011.
[53] See Stewart Goetz and Charles Taliaferro, *Naturalism* (Eerdmans, 2008) and *A Brief History of the Soul* (Wiley-Blackwell, 2011).
[54] Lewis, *Miracles*, 33.   [55] Lewis, *Miracles*, 43.

The beginnings of an answer to the first question are found in Lewis's belief that each of us knows himself better than anything else: 'There is one thing, and only one, in the whole universe which we know more about than we could learn from external observation. That one thing is Man. We do not merely observe men, we *are* men. In this case we have, so to speak, inside information; we are in the know.'[56]

The argument from reason draws upon our direct awareness of the mental events involved in our reasoning. Beyond the fact that we know that we reason, what else did Lewis think we know about ourselves? From the fact that we reason, he believed we know that we are entities or substances which are capable of and do endure as *numerically identical* or as *the numerically same things* through time.[57] Using a series of sensations instead of a sequence of thoughts as his example, Lewis wrote the following to explain how we know we are substances which endure as the same entity through change:

> Suppose that three sensations follow one another – first A, then B, then C. When this happens to you, you have the experience of passing through the process ABC. But note what this implies. It implies that there is something in you which stands sufficiently outside A to notice A passing away, and sufficiently outside B to notice B now beginning and coming to fill the place which A has vacated; and something which recognizes itself as the same through the transition from A to B and B to C, so it can say 'I have had the experience of ABC'. Now this something is what I call Consciousness or Soul... The simplest experience of ABC as a succession demands a soul which is not itself a mere succession of states, but rather a permanent bed along which these different portions of the stream of sensation roll, and which recognizes itself as the same beneath them all.[58]

We are aware that we are substances. If we replace A with A > B, B with B > C, and C with A > C, why did Lewis believe the substance in which the apprehensions of A > B, B > C, and A > C follow each other is a soul and not, say, a material atom? After all, Lewis said that the purpose of his argument from reason was to establish the distinction between reason and nature and not between soul and body or mind and matter.[59] Part of the answer to this question

---

[56] C. S. Lewis, *Mere Christianity* (HarperSanFrancisco, [1952] 2001), 23.
[57] Numerical identity or sameness contrasts with qualitative identity or sameness. For example, Ford Motor Company can manufacture two or more numerically distinct trucks which are qualitatively identical (i.e., trucks that have the same color, body, tires, engine, etc.). It is each truck's numerical identity that explains it being numerically distinct from other individual trucks, while each individual truck is qualitatively the same as the other individual trucks.
[58] Lewis, *The Problem of Pain*, 135.
[59] Lewis, *Miracles*, 38. Though Lewis claimed in *Miracles* that the purpose of his argument from reason was to establish the falsity of naturalism and not to distinguish between soul and body, he nevertheless believed that the argument from reason did establish the distinction. For example, he also wrote the following in *Miracles*: '[I]f [man] were [nothing but a Natural organism], then, as we have seen, all thoughts would be equally nonsensical, for all would have [nonrational]

is found in comments Lewis made about the nature of the mental events involved in reasoning. Lewis maintained that reasoning cannot occur in anything that is material in nature because of the intrinsic aboutness or intentionality of what is mental in nature. According to Lewis, 'a complete philosophy must get in *all* the facts [and] one of the facts total thought must think about is Thinking itself'.[60] And when we think about thinking itself, it is clear that our thoughts are not material or physical (Lewis used the terms interchangeably) in nature because 'physical events, as such, cannot in any intelligible sense be said to be [intrinsically] "about" or to "refer to" anything'.[61] '[T]o talk of one bit of matter as being [intrinsically] true about another bit of matter seems to me to be nonsense'.[62] While what is mental is often about a bit of matter (one can think, hope, desire, etc., about things in the material world), it cannot itself be material in nature. As Lewis wrote in his diary in 1922, 'mind and body' constitute an 'antithesis'.[63]

1.6 Natural-Born Dualists

The intentionality of the mental provides part of the answer to the question about why Lewis believed each of us is a soul.[64] But this part of the answer, like the argument from reason, is inferential and philosophical in nature and hardly one of which an ordinary person is cognizant. Nevertheless, as I have already pointed out at the outset of this section, Lewis thought ordinary people non-inferentially believe that they are souls which have material bodies. For example, Lewis wrote the following about Jews and early Christians:

> From the earliest times the Jews, like many other nations, had believed that man possessed a 'soul' or *Nephesh* separable from the body, which went at death into the shadowy world called *Sheol:* a land of forgetfulness and imbecility where none called upon Jehovah any more, a land half unreal and melancholy like the Hades of the Greeks or the Niflheim of the

---

causes. Man must therefore be a composite being – a natural organism tenanted by, or in a state of *symbiosis* with, a supernatural spirit' (Lewis, *Miracles*, 204). Elsewhere, in a presentation of his argument from reason, Lewis wrote that 'our minds ... claim to be spirit', and we 'must draw the conclusion that we are *not derived from* [this universe]. We are strangers here. We come from somewhere else.... There is "another world," and that is where we come from' (C. S. Lewis, 'On Living in an Atomic Age', in *Present Concerns: A Compelling Collection of Timely, Journalistic Essays*, ed. Walter Hooper (Harcourt, [1948] in 1986), 77–8). On the idea of our coming from somewhere else, see Section 3 on belief that God exists.

[60] Lewis, *Miracles*, 65.   [61] Lewis, *The Discarded Image*, 166.
[62] C. S. Lewis, 'De Futilitate', in *Christian Reflections*, ed. Walter Hooper (Eerdmans, 1967), 64.
[63] Lewis, *All My Road before Me*, 72. Lewis's interest in the philosophical importance of the soul's existence was evidenced in 1924 with his consideration of pursuing doctoral work at Oxford on the Cambridge Platonist Henry More (281; see also Lewis, *The Collected Letters, Volume I*, 623).
[64] As I will point out in Section 2, it is reasonable to hold that Lewis believed being a mind is sufficient, but might not be necessary, for being a soul.

Norsemen. From it shades could return and appear to the living, as Samuel's shade had done at the command of the Witch of Endor.[65]

[Early Christians] believed in [ghosts] so firmly that, on more than one occasion, Christ had had to assure them that He was *not* a ghost.[66]

Jews and early Christians believed in what is known amongst academics as soul-body dualism (dualism, for short). The experimental cognitive scientist Jesse Bering acknowledges that human beings are believers in dualism,[67] and the psychologist Nicholas Humphrey makes clear that there is a non-inferential human inclination to believe in dualism.[68] He cites other scholars who also make this point:

> Thus, development psychologist Paul Bloom aptly describes human beings as 'natural-born dualists'. Anthropologist Alfred Gell writes: 'It seems that ordinary human beings are "natural dualists," inclined more or less from day one, to believe in some kind of "ghost in the machine" …' Neuropsychologist Paul Broks writes: 'The separateness of body and mind is a primordial intuition… Human beings are natural born soul makers, adept at extracting unobservable minds from the behaviour of observable bodies, including their own'.[69]

Lewis maintained the non-inferential belief of ordinary people in the existence of souls and bodies provides the intellectual framework for a non-inferential belief in the presence of spirits in other material objects which is found at a very early period in human history: 'At the outset the universe appears packed with will, intelligence, life and positive qualities; every tree is a nymph and every planet a god. Man himself is akin to the gods'.[70] Not surprisingly, Lewis was convinced that a belief in naturalism led to a disenchantment, a de-souling, of not only ourselves but also, before us, of the universe:

> The advance of knowledge gradually empties this rich and genial universe: first of its gods, then of its colours, smells, sounds and tastes, finally of solidity itself as solidity was originally imagined. As these items are taken from the world, they are transferred to the subjective side of the account: classified as our sensations, thoughts, images or emotions. The Subject becomes gorged, inflated, at the expense of the Object. But the matter does not rest there. The same method which has emptied the world now proceeds

---

[65] Lewis, *Miracles*, 237.
[66] C. S. Lewis, 'What Are We to Make of Jesus Christ?', in *God in the Dock*, ed. Walter Hooper (Eerdmans, [1950] in 1970), 159.
[67] Jesse Bering, 'The Folk Psychology of Souls', *Behavioral and Brain Sciences* 29 (2006): 453–62.
[68] Nicholas Humphrey, *Soul Dust* (Princeton University Press, 2011).
[69] Humphrey, *Soul Dust*, 195.
[70] C. S. Lewis, 'The Empty Universe', in *Present Concerns: A Compelling Collection of Timely, Journalistic Essays*, ed. Walter Hooper (Harcourt, [1952] in 1986), 81.

to empty ourselves. The masters of the method soon announce that we were just as mistaken (and mistaken in much the same way) when we attributed 'souls', or 'selves' or 'minds' to human organisms, as when we attributed Dryads to the trees. Animism, apparently, begins at home. We, who have personified all other things, turn out to be ourselves mere personifications. Man is indeed akin to the gods: that is, he is no less phantasmal than they. Just as the Dryad is a 'ghost', an abbreviated symbol for all the facts we know about the tree foolishly mistaken for a mysterious entity over and above the facts, so the man's 'mind' or 'consciousness' is an abbreviated symbol for certain verifiable facts about his behaviour: a symbol mistaken for a thing. And just as we have been broken of our bad habit of personifying trees, so we must now be broken of our bad habit of personifying men ... There never was a Subjective account into which we could transfer the items which the Object had lost. There is no 'consciousness' to contain ... all the lost gods, colours, and concepts.[71]

The contemporary psychologist Paul Bloom makes the same point as Lewis about the disenchantment of the world: 'One of the first things an undergraduate learns in an introduction to psychology class is that substance dualism is mistaken. It is assumed by virtually all scientists that mental life is the product of physical brains (though there is little consensus as to *how* this all works). Here, as in other domains, common-sense religious beliefs clash with science'.[72]

Two additional points are relevant here. First, Lewis would have distinguished between science and naturalism and claimed it is the latter and not the former that clashes with a belief in the existence of the soul.[73] Second, Lewis would have disagreed with what seems to be Bloom's assumption that belief in the soul is initially a religious belief. In Section 3, we will see how Lewis's belief that he was a soul *led* him to a religious view of reality. But Lewis would have agreed with Bloom's implicit suggestion that if the belief in substance dualism can be undermined, then religious belief will suffer the same fate.

In defending the existence of the soul, Lewis made clear that he was not advocating a return to animism:

There is of course no question of returning to Animism ... No one supposes that the beliefs of pre-philosophic humanity, just as they stood before they were criticized, can or should be restored. The question is whether the first thinkers in modifying (and rightly modifying) them under the criticism, did not make some rash and unnecessary concession... In emptying out the dryads and the gods (which admittedly, 'would not do' just as they stood)

---

[71] Lewis, 'The Empty Universe', 81–2.
[72] Paul Bloom, 'Religion Is Natural', *Developmental Science* 10 (2007): 149.
[73] Stewart Goetz, *C. S. Lewis* (Wiley-Blackwell, 2018), Chapter 5.

we appear to have thrown out the whole universe, ourselves included. We must go back and begin over again . . .[74]

1.7 The Soul and Happiness

Given Lewis's defence of the integrity of our reasoning, one might be tempted to conclude that he believed reasoning is what life is all about, that reasoning is ultimately what makes life worth living. However, Lewis did not believe this. He wrote that 'I doubt if I'd care for [a planet] of pure intelligence' but 'I'm all for a planet without aches or pains'.[75] For Lewis, aches and pains were one of two primary loci of intrinsic value, the other locus of value being pleasure. In the next section, I set forth Lewis's treatment of pleasure and pain, happiness, and what makes life worth living.

2 The Pleasure that Makes Life Worth Living

2.1 The Intrinsic Goodness of Pleasure

Lewis wrote, '[l]et the doctor tell me I shall die, unless I do so-and-so; but whether life is worth having on those terms is no more a question for him than for any other man'.[76] What did Lewis believe makes life worth having or living? He thought what makes life worth living is what is good, and he believed '"Life" in the biological sense has nothing to do with good and evil until sentience appears'.[77] What is it about sentience that Lewis believed has something to do with good and evil? The short answer is that Lewis thought the relevance of sentience for good and evil was located in experiences of pleasure and pain, because it is the natures of pleasure and pain that ultimately explain good and evil. The long answer details what Lewis thought about the nature of the relationships between pleasure and goodness and pain and evilness. To understand the nature of these relationships, I turn to the notion of an intrinsic property.

What is an intrinsic property? If Y is an intrinsic property of X, then X does not have Y in virtue of X's relationship to something else. That is, X has Y independently of X's relationship to anything else. X has Y in and of itself. The logical opposite of an intrinsic property is an extrinsic property. Not surprisingly, if Y is an extrinsic property of X, then X has Y in virtue of X's relationship to something else. X does not have Y in and of itself. Lewis believed that an experience of pleasure is intrinsically good. That is, Lewis

---

[74] Lewis, 'The Empty Universe', 85. [75] Lewis, *The Collected Letters, Volume III*, 623.
[76] C. S. Lewis, 'Is Progress Possible?', in *God in the Dock*, ed. Walter Hooper (Eerdmans, [1958] in 1970), 315.
[77] Lewis, *The Problem of Pain*, 133.

believed an experience of pleasure is good independently of that experience's relationship to anything else. Lewis thought an experience of pleasure is good in and of itself: 'I have no doubt at all that pleasure is in itself a good'.[78] '[A]ll pleasure [is] simply good'.[79] (NB: Because Lewis believed pleasure is not the only intrinsic good, he was not a hedonist, a point to which I shall return later in this section.)

Because Lewis believed pleasure is intrinsically good, he considered the development of taste for a different food to be a form of growth: 'where I formerly had only one pleasure, I now have two'.[80] Because he thought pleasure is intrinsically good, he believed its goodness provided a person with a reason to pursue the experience of it for its own sake. However, Lewis also acknowledged that there are situations in which one ought not to pursue an experience of pleasure. For example, a moral consideration can give a person a reason not to pursue pleasure on a certain occasion (see the final subsection of this section). What Lewis thought was conceptually incoherent was a person having a reason to deny himself an experience of pleasure for its own sake or simply because it is an experience of pleasure. Lewis believed Christians were frequently confused about this issue, and he commented on this confusion in terms of the concept of unselfishness:

> If you asked twenty good men today what they thought the highest of the virtues, nineteen of them would reply, Unselfishness. But if you had asked almost any of the great Christians of old, he would have replied, Love. You see what has happened? A negative term has been substituted for a positive, and this is of more than philological importance. The negative idea of Unselfishness carries with it the suggestion not primarily of securing good things for others, but of going without them ourselves, as if our abstinence and not their happiness was the important point. I do not think this is the Christian virtue of Love. The New Testament has lots to say about self-denial, but not about self-denial as an end in itself.[81]

When a person ought not to pursue an experience of pleasure for himself, the happiness of others can be the reason for doing so. Self-denial for its own sake cannot be the reason. Lewis wrote to Joan Lancaster that '*of course* you are quite right if you mean that giving up fun for no reason except that you think it's "good" to give it up, is all nonsense'.[82] Lewis was so convinced that

---

[78] C. S. Lewis, 'Christianity and Culture', in *Christian Reflections*, ed. Walter Hooper (Eerdmans, 1967), 21.
[79] Lewis, *The Collected Letters, Volume II*, 462.
[80] C. S. Lewis, 'On Three Ways of Writing for Children', in *On Stories and Other Essays on Literature*, ed. Walter Hooper (Harcourt, [1952] in 1982), 34.
[81] C. S. Lewis, 'The Weight of Glory', in *The Weight of Glory and Other Addresses*, ed. Walter Hooper (HarperCollins, [1941] in 2001), 25.
[82] Lewis, *The Collected Letters, Volume III*, 871.

unselfishness and/or sacrifice of pleasure for its own sake cannot be a reason for forgoing an experience of pleasure that he had the devilish Screwtape in *The Screwtape Letters* instruct his nephew Wormwood to 'teach a man to surrender benefits not that others may be happy in having them [which is the right reason for the surrender] but that he may be unselfish in forgoing them [which is the wrong reason for the surrender]'.[83] When a person is interested in rightly restraining himself in the pursuit of pleasure, he is concerned with not unjustly interfering with the opportunities of others to experience their own happiness.

But, one might be thinking, surely there are bad pleasures. Lewis thought there are pleasures which are extrinsically bad, but none which is intrinsically evil. He wrote that 'bad pleasures' is shorthand for

> 'pleasures snatched by [morally] unlawful acts'. It is the stealing of the apple that is bad, not the sweetness [the pleasure]. The sweetness is still a beam from the glory. That does not palliate the stealing. It makes it worse. There is sacrilege in the theft. We have abused a holy thing [the pleasure] ... [and ignored] the smell of Deity that hangs about it.[84]
>
> [W]hat we call bad pleasures are pleasures produced by actions, or inactions, [which] break the moral law, and it is those actions or inactions [which] are [intrinsically] bad, not the pleasures.[85]

Lewis maintained that pleasure is intrinsically good. What, if anything, did he think is intrinsically evil or bad? Given what he believed about the intrinsic goodness of pleasure, it is not surprising that he believed an experience of pain is intrinsically evil. He thought an experience of pain is evil independently of its relationship to anything else. 'I have no doubt at all that ... pain in itself [is] an evil'.[86] 'Pain is unmasked, unmistakable evil'.[87]

Is all pain intrinsically bad? Lewis thought so on the conceptual grounds that if pain *per se* is intrinsically evil, then any pain is intrinsically evil. In discussing the issue of vivisection, he wrote that

> if pain is not an evil, why should human suffering be reduced? We must therefore assume as a basis of the whole discussion [of vivisection] that pain is an evil, otherwise there is nothing to be discussed... If we find a man giving pleasure it is for us to prove (if we criticise him) that his action is wrong. But if we find a man inflicting pain it is for him to prove that his action is right'.[88]

---

[83] C. S. Lewis, *The Screwtape Letters and Screwtape Proposes a Toast* (Macmillan, 1961), 121.
[84] Lewis, *Letters to Malcolm*, 89, 90. The smell of deity hangs about pleasure because God is happy. See the end of the subsection 'Eudaimonism' in this section.
[85] Lewis, *The Collected Letters, Volume II*, 462–3.   [86] Lewis, 'Christianity and Culture', 21.
[87] Lewis, *The Problem of Pain*, 90.
[88] C. S. Lewis, 'Vivisection', in *God in the Dock*, ed. Walter Hooper (Eerdmans, [1947] in 1970), 224–5.

Because Lewis believed pain is intrinsically evil, he thought it differs from things like 'meat, or beer, or the cinema' which '[a]n individual Christian may see fit to give up ... for special reasons ... [B]ut the moment he starts saying [these] things are bad in themselves ... he has taken the wrong turning'.[89] Because pain is intrinsically evil, Lewis insisted a person has a reason to avoid pain for its own sake. When grieving the death of his wife, Joy Davidman, he wrote, '[b]ut we are not at all – if we understand ourselves – seeking the aches for their own sake'.[90] And while discussing the existence and nature of purgatory as purification, he commented, 'I assume the process of purification will normally involve suffering... But I don't think suffering is the purpose of the purgation'.[91] The idea that a person can have a reason to pursue what is intrinsically bad for its own sake is incoherent. Lewis believed people might think they can have a reason to pursue what is bad for its own sake in light of their consideration of the idea of cruelty. But he insisted that 'cruelty does not come from desiring evil as such'.[92] Rather, cruelty is explained by the desire for pleasure. Certain persons 'take pleasure in making other people uncomfortable',[93] and the worst ways of getting pleasure's goodness involve power over and hatred of others.[94] In sum,

> we have no experience of anyone liking badness just because it is bad. The nearest we can get to it is in cruelty. But in real life people are cruel for one of two reasons – either because they are sadists, that is, because they have a sexual perversion which makes cruelty a cause of sensual pleasure to them, or else for the sake of something they are going to get out of it – money, or power, or safety. But pleasure, money, power, and safety are all, as far as they go, good things. The badness consists in pursuing them by the wrong method, or in the wrong way, or too much. I do not mean, of course, that the people who do this are not desperately wicked. I do mean that wickedness, when you examine it, turns out to be the pursuit of some good in the wrong way. You can be good for the sake of goodness: you cannot be bad for the mere sake of badness... [N]o one ever did a cruel action simply because cruelty is wrong – only because cruelty was pleasant or useful to him... In order to be bad he must have good things to want and then to pursue in the wrong way.[95]

Lewis believed pleasure is intrinsically good, yet he understood that people often wrongly feel guilty when they licitly experience it because it is frequently

---

[89] Lewis, *Mere Christianity*, 79, 78–9.
[90] C. S. Lewis, *A Grief Observed* (HarperSanFrancisco, [1961] 2001), 54.
[91] Lewis, *Letters to Malcolm*, 109.   [92] Lewis, 'Evil and God', 23.
[93] Lewis, *Mere Christianity*, 95.   [94] Lewis, *Mere Christianity*, 102–3.
[95] Lewis, *Mere Christianity*, 43–4. Lewis also believed our loves for people are ultimately conceptually linked with pleasure because they stand on our elementary likings. '[A]nd since to "like" anything means to take some sort of pleasure in it, [to understand our loves] we must begin with pleasure'. Lewis, *The Four Loves*, 10.

gotten through immoral actions. When the main character, Elwin Ransom, a Christian philologist, arrived on the planet Venus in *Perelandra* (the second book of Lewis's space trilogy), he had

> the strange sense of excessive pleasure which seemed somehow to be communicated to him through all of his senses at once. I use the word 'excessive' because Ransom himself could only describe it by saying that for his first few days on Perelandra he was haunted, not by a feeling of guilt, but by surprise that he had no such feeling. There was an exuberance or prodigality of sweetness about the mere act of living which our race finds it difficult not to associate with forbidden and extravagant actions.[96]

In light of what follows in this section, it will be helpful to provide a brief explanation about the difference between the nature of experiences of pleasure (and pain) and that of mental events like thought, belief, desire, hope, choice, and so on which I discussed in Section 1.2. There I discussed how an event is mental in nature if it has intentionality or aboutness. Experiences of pleasure are *not* mental in nature because they have no aboutness. While we experience pleasure from, say, thinking about a beautiful sunset, the pleasure itself is not about the sunset. In ordinary language, we might say I am pleased about the beautiful sunset. However, this means we get pleasure from our thoughts about the sunset. In order to distinguish experiences like pleasure and pain from mental events, philosophers term the former *qualia*, which is the plural form of the Latin word *quale* which means 'of a sort or kind'. Both *qualia* and mental events are plausibly regarded as psychological in nature, where the psychological is a genus of which *qualia* and mental events are species. It is helpful to remember that the term 'psychological' comes from the Greek word 'psuché', which means 'soul'. Given Lewis's concern with justifying the pain suffered by seemingly non-self-conscious animals in vivisection,[97] it is reasonable to conclude he believed having either a qualitative capacity (e.g., the capacity to experience pleasure) or a propositional-attitude capacity (e.g., the capacity to think) was sufficient for being a soul, but being a soul might not be sufficient for being a mind in the sense specified in Section 1.2.

Just as Lewis thought that ordinary people believe in the existence of the soul and substance dualism, he was also convinced that the view that pleasure is intrinsically good is 'the normal value judgement of all unsophisticated people'.[98] However, as with substance dualism, the belief that pleasure is

---

[96] C. S. Lewis, *Perelandra* (Scribner, [1944] 2003), 33.   [97] Lewis, 'Vivisection'.
[98] Lewis, *The Collected Letters, Volume II*, 463.

intrinsically good is something which philosophers either reject or 'are always neglecting'.[99] The philosopher Jaegwon Kim made the following comments about the ordinary and philosophical attitudes about consciousness generally and pleasure particularly:

> For most of us [unsophisticated people], there is no need to belabor the centrality of consciousness to our conception of ourselves as creatures with minds. But I want to point to the ambivalent, almost paradoxical, attitude that philosophers have displayed toward consciousness... [C]onsciousness had been virtually banished from the philosophical and scientific scene for much of the last century, and consciousness-bashing still goes on in some quarters, with some reputable philosophers arguing that phenomenal consciousness, or 'qualia', is a fiction of bad philosophy. And there are philosophers ... who, while they recognize phenomenal consciousness as something real, do not believe that a complete science of human behavior, including cognitive psychology and neuroscience, has a place for consciousness ... in an explanatory/predictive theory of cognition and behavior.[100]

Kim's claim about consciousness-bashing hearkens back to naturalism which in principle excludes the mental from the explanatory story concerning the occurrences of material events in this world. Kim further differentiated between the status of consciousness among philosophers and its place in ordinary life:

> Contrast this lowly status of consciousness in science and metaphysics with its lofty standing in moral philosophy and value theory. When philosophers discuss the nature of the intrinsic good, or what is worthy of our desire and volition for its own sake, the most prominently mentioned candidates are things like pleasure, absence of pain, enjoyment, and happiness... To most of us, a fulfilling life, a life worth living, is one that is rich and full in qualitative consciousness. We would regard life as impoverished and not fully satisfying if it never included experiences of things like the smell of the sea in a cool morning breeze, the lambent play of sunlight on brilliant autumn foliage, the fragrance of a field of lavender in bloom, and the vibrant, layered soundscape projected by a string quartet... It is an ironic fact that the felt qualities of conscious experience, perhaps the only things that ultimately matter to us, are often relegated in the rest of philosophy to the status of 'secondary qualities', in the shadowy zone between the real and the unreal, or even jettisoned outright as artifacts of confused minds.[101]

According to Kim, when philosophers discuss the nature of what is intrinsically good, the most prominent candidates are the qualitative experiences of pleasure

---

[99] Lewis, *The Collected Letters, Volume II*, 463.
[100] Jaegwon Kim, *Physicalism, or Something Near Enough* (Princeton University Press, 2005), 10–11.
[101] Kim, *Physicalism, or Something Near Enough*, 11–12.

which constitute happiness. It is these which Kim claims most of us (ordinary people) believe matter most and make life worth living. Lewis agreed. He wrote about mental images that

> in their total effect ... mediate to me something very important. It is always something qualitative – more like an adjective than a noun. That, for me, gives it the impact of reality. For I think we respect nouns (and what we think they stand for) too much. All my deepest, and certainly all my earliest, experiences seem to be of sheer quality... If a musical phrase could be translated into words at all it would become an adjective. A great lyric is very like a long, utterly adequate, adjective. Plato was not so silly as the Moderns think when he elevated abstract nouns – that is, adjectives disguised as nouns – into the supreme realities – the Forms.[102]

2.2 Eudaimonism

Philosophers, writes Kim, believe everyday people are confused. Do philosophers, then, fail to recognize anything of value? Those who do not jettison value completely, at least in words, usually advocate what is commonly known in the academy as virtue theory (in this context, virtues are traits such as patience, steadfastness, and benevolence) or eudaimonism. 'Eudaimonism' derives from the Greek word 'eudaimōn', which literally means 'good spirit' and is commonly thought of as happiness. According to the philosopher Nicholas Wolterstorff,

> [t]he eudaimonist holds that ... the well-lived life [is], by definition, the happy life, the *eudaimōn* life... It is important to understand what sort of goal happiness is [according to the eudaimonist]. 'Happiness' is not the name of experience of a certain sort. 'Pleasure' names experiences of a certain sort; 'happiness' does not. The eudaimonist is not saying that one's sole end in itself is or should be bringing about experiences of a certain sort, everything else being a means... [T]he ancient eudaimonists insisted that *eudaimonia* is activity. Happiness does not consist in what happens to one but in what one makes of what happens to one.[103]

In light of Wolterstorff's remarks, there are two considerations indicating that Lewis did not espouse eudaimonism.

First, there are Lewis's own statements about the intrinsic goodness of pleasure and the intrinsic evilness of pain which I have already quoted. When read straightforwardly, these statements support the view that Lewis thought of happiness as experiences of pleasure. Indeed, anyone who takes the time to

---

[102] Lewis, *Letters to Malcolm*, 86.
[103] Nicholas Wolterstorff, *Justice: Rights and Wrongs* (Princeton University Press, 2008), 150, 151, 152.

carefully read Lewis's many writings cannot help but notice how often he mentions and discusses pleasure and pain, and how when he mentions pleasure he slides over to talking about happiness, or *vice versa*. Here, a few examples will have to suffice. In recounting his early life in *Surprised by Joy*, Lewis wrote that '[w]ith my mother's death all settled happiness ... disappeared from my life. There was to be much fun, many pleasures ... but no more of the old security'.[104] About Jane Austen, Lewis wrote that "[s]he has, or at least all her favourite characters have, a hearty relish for what would now be regarded as very modest pleasures. A ball, a dinner party, books, conversation, a drive to see a great house ten miles away, a holiday as far as Derbyshire – these ... are happiness."[105] And in a short essay entitled 'Hedonics', Lewis used the words 'pleasure', 'happiness', and 'joy' interchangeably.[106]

Those who either completely neglect or give passing mention to Lewis's thoughts about happiness sometimes mistakenly take his mention of virtue as sufficient for his being a eudaimonist. For example, Adam Barkman writes that 'Lewis agreed with Plato (and ... also with Aristotle) that although virtue is a means to happiness, it is also an essential part of happiness ... True Happiness always requires virtue'.[107] The problem here is that, while Lewis did believe both that perfect happiness requires virtue in the sense that only those who justly choose a virtuous life should experience the perfect happiness that is essential to a heavenly life, and that once in heaven they will get pleasure from the activity which flows from their virtuous character, Lewis never stated (and Barkman never provides a reference where he stated) that virtuous activity is an essential *part of* happiness. At one point, Barkman claims that eudaimonism is the view that 'makes the desire for happiness [conceptually] prior to duty to the moral law'.[108] If someone who believes this general statement qualifies as a eudaimonist, then Lewis was a eudaimonist. But a person can believe this statement without believing that activity of any kind (including virtuous activity) is an essential part of happiness, which Wolterstorff and Barkman (at other points in his discussion of Lewis's thought) correctly maintain is the belief of a eudaimonist.

Second, Lewis was commonsensical, and his conception of happiness is that of ordinary people while the eudaimonist's understanding of happiness is not.

---

[104] Lewis, *Surprised by Joy*, 21.
[105] C. S. Lewis, 'A Note on Jane Austen', in *Selected Literary Essays*, ed. Walter Hooper (Cambridge University Press, [1954] in 1969), 185–6.
[106] C. S. Lewis, 'Hedonics', in *Present Concerns: A Compelling Collection of Timely, Journalistic Essays*, ed. Walter Hooper (Harcourt, [1945] in 1986), 50–5.
[107] Adam Barkman, *C. S. Lewis & Philosophy as a Way of Life* (Zossima Press, 2009), 395.
[108] Barkman, *C. S. Lewis & Philosophy as a Way of Life*, 322.

The eudaimonist philosopher Julia Annas has this to say about ancient eudaimonist theories vis-à-vis common sense:

> [A]ncient [eudaimonistic] theories are all more or less revisionary, and some of them are highly counterintuitive. They give an account of happiness which, if baldly presented to a non-philosopher without any of the supporting arguments, sounds wrong, even absurd... [A]ncient theories greatly expand and modify the ordinary non-philosophical understanding of happiness, opening themselves up to criticism from non-philosophers on this score.
>
> It is in fact common ground to the ancient theories that, on the one hand, we are all right to assume that our final end is happiness of some kind, and to try to achieve happiness in reflecting systematically on our final end; but that, on the other hand, we are very far astray in our initial assumptions about what happiness is... So we should not be surprised that ancient theories have counter-intuitive consequences about happiness.[109]

When I discuss Lewis's view of pleasure and pain with others, many of them immediately respond with, 'That's hedonism!', which bespeaks their implicit assumption that no one could ever reasonably espouse belief in the intrinsic goodness of pleasure and the intrinsic evilness of pain without being a hedonist. However, contrary to what these individuals think, Lewis's view is strictly speaking *not* an espousal of hedonism. In philosophical terms, hedonism is the view that there is one, *and only one*, intrinsic good, and one, *and only one*, intrinsic evil. While Lewis believed pleasure is intrinsically good and pain is intrinsically evil, he did *not* believe pleasure is the only intrinsic good and pain is the only intrinsic evil. 'We have had enough, once and for all, of Hedonism – the gloomy philosophy which says that Pleasure is the only good'.[110]

I will turn to what Lewis thought about an additional intrinsic good and evil in a moment. At present, it is important to make clear what Lewis did not and did affirm about hedonism as strictly understood. While he denied the truth of hedonism, he affirmed a hedonistic understanding of happiness. That is, like a hedonist, Lewis believed that happiness consists of experiences of pleasure, and perfect happiness, were it to exist, would consist of nothing but experiences of pleasure (there would be no experience of pain). He took the identification of happiness with pleasure to be so obvious that he never argued for it, though he conveyed in writing that his view of pleasure and happiness was hedonistic in nature. When discussing his book, *The Problem of Pain*, Lewis wrote that 'I wasn't writing on the Problem of Pleasure! If I had been you might find my views *too* hedonistic'.[111] Even God, in Lewis's view, is a hedonist about happiness:

---

[109] Julia Annas, *The Morality of Happiness* (Oxford University Press, 1993), 331.
[110] Lewis, 'Hedonics', 54–5. [111] Lewis, *The Collected Letters, Volume II*, 463.

All those fasts and vigils and stakes and crosses are only a façade. Or only like foam on the seashore. Out at sea, out in His sea, there is pleasure, and more pleasure. He makes no secret of it; at His right hand are 'pleasures for evermore [which is a quote of Psalm 16: 11]' ... He's vulgar ... He has a bourgeois mind.[112]

For Lewis, the Trinity is
The Happy Trinity[113]

2.3 The Explanation of Morality

In *Perelandra*, Lewis says the king of Perelandra was taught about 'evil and good, of anguish and joy'.[114] On Lewis's understanding of value, to learn about good and evil is first and foremost to learn about the *non-moral* intrinsic good and intrinsic evil of pleasure and pain respectively. Only then can one learn about *moral* good and evil, because moral good and evil are conceptually derivative forms of value which require the existence of non-moral value. In other words, Lewis believed that it is metaphysically necessary that moral good and evil could not exist without qualitative good and evil, because the existence of the latter provides the explanation for the existence of the former.

Justin Buckley Dyer and Micah J. Watson rightly recognize that Lewis had a 'strong commitment to natural law'[115] in the sense that he took moral principles – the core of which Lewis maintained is expressed in what he called the 'Tao' in *The Abolition of Man* – to be grounded in the nature of human beings. Lewis wrote that 'classical moralists after the style of Thomas Aquinas, Grotius, Hooker, and Locke [believe] that behind the laws of the state there is a Natural Law... I agree ... I hold this conception to be basic to all civilization'.[116]

But what is this Natural Law? Lewis wrote that '[God] enjoins what is good because it is good, because He is good. Hence His laws have ... "truth" ... being rooted in His own nature'.[117] A logical question is 'What is God's nature?' Lewis wrote that God 'contains in [Himself] the cause of [His] own and all other bliss ... God gives what He has ... He gives the happiness that there is'.[118] Given Lewis's hedonistic view of happiness, if happiness is part of

---

[112] Lewis, *The Screwtape Letters and Screwtape Proposes a Toast*, 101.
[113] C. S. Lewis, *The Great Divorce* (HarperSanFrancisco, [1946] 2001), 134.
[114] Lewis, *Perelandra*, 180.
[115] Justin Buckley Dyer and Micah Watson, *C. S. Lewis on Politics and the Natural Law* (Cambridge University Press, 2016), p. 15.
[116] C. S. Lewis, 'We Have No Right to Happiness', in *God and the Dock*, ed. Walter Hooper (Eerdmans, [1963] in 1970), 318.
[117] C. S. Lewis, *Reflections on the Psalms* (Harcourt, 1958), 61.
[118] Lewis, *The Problem of Pain*, 40, 47.

God's nature then so is the experience of pleasure with its intrinsic goodness. It is the natures of the *qualia* of pleasure and pain (the experience of which is not part of God's nature) with their respective intrinsic values that Lewis thought gave rise to the natural moral law of good and evil as it pertains to human choices. Lewis recognized that one's own self (soul) as the subject of experiences of pleasure and pain is one among many such selves. And 'it is that one self of all others which [by me] is called *I* and *me* ... [and] which ... puts forward an irrational claim to preference [for happiness]. This claim is to be ... simply killed'[119] in the light of the notion of fair play. 'In the moral sphere, every act of justice ... involves putting ourselves in the other person's place and thus transcending our own competitive particularity'.[120] To choose unjustly one's own happiness at the expense of the happiness of others is unfair. According to Lewis, 'fair play ... between individuals' is the first concern 'when we start thinking about morality'.[121] He wrote that 'in the long run, all men are our brothers',[122] so that rationally

> [w]e 'just see' that there is no reason why my neighbour's happiness should be sacrificed to my own, as we 'just see' that things which are equal to the same thing are equal to one another. If we cannot prove either axiom, that is not because they are irrational but because they are self-evident and all proofs depend on them. Their intrinsic reasonableness shines by its own light. It is because all morality is based on such self-evident principles [e.g., that my neighbour's happiness should not be sacrificed to my own] that we say to a man, when we would call him to right conduct, 'Be reasonable'.[123]

Lewis believed it was in light of the recognition of the intrinsic reasonableness of the self-evident principle that my neighbour's happiness should not be unjustly sacrificed to my own that we derive the Confucian moral demand of 'Do not do to others what you would not like them to do to you' and the Christian moral injunction 'Do as you would be done by'.[124] It is at this point that we encounter what Lewis believed is a second intrinsic good and a second intrinsic evil which are respectively justice and injustice. Because Lewis

---

[119] C. S. Lewis, 'Two Ways with the Self', in *God in the Dock*, ed. Walter Hooper (Eerdmans, [1940] in 1970), 194. For more on Lewis's understanding of dying to self, see the section 'The Christian Myth' in Section 4.
[120] C. S. Lewis, *An Experiment in Criticism* (Cambridge University Press, 1961), 138.
[121] Lewis, *Mere Christianity*, 72.   [122] Lewis, *The Abolition of Man*, 43.
[123] Lewis, *Miracles*, 54.
[124] Lewis, *The Abolition of Man*, 46. See also 'The Divine Command Theory of Morality' in Section 4 of this Element. Lewis implicitly assumed that the principle that my neighbour's happiness should not be sacrificed to my own and the Confucian and Christian imperatives derived from it presupposed the proverbial 'all-other-things-being-equal' clause. For example, the truth of the principle assumes that my neighbour has not forfeited the safeguarding of his happiness against others by himself choosing unjustly in the pursuit of that happiness.

believed justice is intrinsically good and injustice is intrinsically evil, he thought that a person's belief that a certain action is just provides that individual with a reason to choose to perform the action for its own sake. He wrote that 'justice is really good – objectively obligatory whether any one likes it or not'.[125] Similarly, Lewis thought that a person who believed a certain action was unjust provided that individual with a reason to choose not to perform the action for its own sake. In a discussion of the difference in views between a materialistic hedonist who believes in the maximization of happiness for as many people as possible and a Christian who does not believe this, Lewis wrote the following: '[W]here the Materialist would simply ask about a proposed action "Will it increase the happiness of the majority?", the Christian might have to say, "Even if it does increase the happiness of the majority, we can't do it. It is unjust."'[126] '[T]he inflexible demands of justice',[127] thought Lewis, provide the Christian with a reason to choose not to perform a certain action because injustice is intrinsically evil. It is, thought Lewis, a 'higher claim' and men who choose to surrender to it will 'pursue their own interests no further than this claim will allow'.[128]

2.4 Pleasures as Shafts of Divine Glory

As I turn in Section 3 to an examination of why Lewis believed in God, it is fitting to link his view of pleasure and its intrinsic goodness with his belief in the existence of God. He reminded his readers that when one believes in God's existence, one can worship and adore. But what object might one use for assistance in beginning to worship and adore God? In *Letters to Malcolm*, Lewis wrote to the hypothetical interlocutor, Malcolm, that

> [y]ou first taught me the great principle 'Begin where you are'.... You turned to the brook and once more splashed your burning face and hands in the little waterfall and said, 'Why not begin with this?'
> And it worked. Apparently you have never guessed how much. That cushiony moss, that coldness and sound and dancing light were no doubt very minor blessings compared with 'the means of grace and the hope of

---

[125] Lewis, 'De Futilitate', 67.
[126] C. S. Lewis, 'Man or Rabbit?', in *God in the Dock*, ed. Walter Hooper (Eerdmans, [1946?] in 1970), 109.
[127] Lewis, *The Abolition of Man*, 43.
[128] C. S. Lewis, 'Three Kinds of Men', in *Present Concerns: A Compelling Collection of Timely, Journalistic Essays*, ed. Walter Hooper (Harcourt, [1943] in 1986), 21. Utilitarianism is a version of hedonism, and the utilitarian John Stuart Mill wrote of justice that it poses 'the only real difficulty in the utilitarian theory of morals'. John Stuart Mill, 'Utilitarianism', in *Selected Writings of John Stuart Mill*, ed. Maurice Cowling (New York: Mentor, 1968), 304. Though a hedonist about happiness, Lewis was not a hedonist because of his belief that justice is intrinsically good.

glory'... They were not the hope of glory, they were an exposition of the glory itself.

Yet you were not – or so it seemed to me – telling me that 'Nature', or 'the beauties of Nature', manifest the glory. No such abstraction as 'Nature' comes into it. I was learning the far more secret doctrine that *pleasures* are shafts of the glory as it strikes our sensibility. As it impinges on our will or our understanding, we give it different names – goodness or truth or the like. But its flash upon our senses and mood is pleasure.[129]

3 Belief that God Exists

3.1 The Numinous: Non-Inferential Quasi-Religious Belief

According to Lewis, there are 'three strands or elements'[130] in all developed religions. In the light of his conviction that everyone starts out with a non-inferential belief that he is a soul, Lewis claimed that the first element in any developed religion is a 'potentially or implicitly religious [or] *quasi-religious*'[131] experience or feeling of the numinous (of the spiritual or, perhaps, divine) when beholding the natural world. 'This feeling', wrote Lewis, 'may be described as awe, and the object which excites it as the *Numinous*'.[132] In the

> region of awe ... in deepest solitude there is a road right out of the self, a commerce with something which, by refusing to identity itself with any object of the senses, or anything whereof we have biological or social need, or anything imagined, or any state of our own minds, proclaims itself sheerly objective. Far more objective than bodies, for it is not, like them, clothed in our senses; the naked Other, imageless (though our imagination salutes it with a hundred images), unknown, undefined, desired.[133]

Lewis wrote that we find many examples of the experience of the numinous in nature mentioned in literature:

> Going back about a century we find copious examples in Wordsworth – perhaps the finest being that passage in the first book of the *Prelude* where he describes his experience while rowing on the lake in the stolen boat. Going back further we get a very pure and strong example in Malory, when Galahad 'began to tremble right hard when the deadly (=mortal) flesh began to behold the spiritual things'... In Pagan literature we find Ovid's picture of the dark grove on the Aventine of which you would say at a glance *numen inest* – the place is haunted, or there is a Presence here.[134]

---

[129] Lewis, *Letters to Malcolm*, 88–9.   [130] Lewis, *The Problem of Pain*, 5.
[131] C. S. Lewis, 'Is Theism Important?', in *God in the Dock*, ed. Walter Hooper (Eerdmans, [1952] in 1970), 174.
[132] Lewis, *The Problem of Pain*, 6.   [133] Lewis, *Surprised by Joy*, 221.
[134] Lewis, *The Problem of Pain*, 7.

In the light of each person's belief that he is a soul with a material body and his experience of the numinous in the natural world which, like his body, is material, 'man, from a very early period, began to believe that the universe was haunted by spirits'.[135]

Lewis believed the second strand in any developed religion is a non-inferential belief in

> some kind of morality; that is, [men] feel towards certain proposed actions the experiences expressed by the words 'I ought' or 'I ought not'. These experiences resemble awe in one respect, namely that they cannot be logically deduced from the environment and physical experiences of the man who undergoes them... Morality ... goes beyond anything that can be 'given' in the facts of experience.[136]

The third stage in religious development, thought Lewis, arises when men bring together the numinous and morality, 'when the Numinous Power to which they feel awe is made the guardian of the morality to which they feel obligation'.[137] This linking is 'natural to humanity' even though 'it fulfils no one's wishes'.[138]

Every developed religion has these three elements, according to Lewis. What did he think led from the three shared elements of any religion to explicitly theistic religious belief in the existence of God? At this point, Lewis thought we turn to inference.

3.2 I Exist and Inferential Belief that God Exists

Lewis wrote that 'man even at his highest ... intelligence has no direct "knowledge about" ... the ultimate Being ... Statements about God are extrapolations from the knowledge of other things'.[139] As we know from Section 1, Lewis believed the naturalist cannot disenchant us through reasoning because reasoning itself is enchanted. We also know that Lewis believed reasoning occurs in the soul. Lewis thought that the most important other thing of which we have knowledge and from which we extrapolate or infer knowledge of God's existence is the soul.

What is the explanation of my existence? I might understand this as a question about the *purpose* of my existence. Lewis believed that if I understand the question this way, then I am thinking of myself as something that is made or created. Lewis opened his book *A Preface to Paradise Lost* with the following words:

---

[135] Lewis, *The Problem of Pain*, 6.   [136] Lewis, *The Problem of Pain*, 10–11.
[137] Lewis, *The Problem of Pain*, 11–12.   [138] Lewis, *The Problem of Pain*, 12.
[139] Lewis, *The Four Loves*, 126.

> The first qualification for judging any piece of workmanship from a corkscrew to a cathedral is to know *what* it is – what it was intended to do and how it is meant to be used. After that has been discovered the temperance reformer may decide that the corkscrew was made for a bad purpose, and the communist may think the same about the cathedral. But such questions come later. The first thing is to understand the object before you: as long as you think the corkscrew was meant for opening tins or the cathedral for entertaining tourists you can say nothing to the purpose about them. The first thing the reader needs to know about *Paradise Lost* is what Milton meant it to be.[140]

In summary, in asking for the explanation of my existence, I might be asking about what I am in the sense of what I am supposed to do, how I am supposed to function, in virtue of my being an entity or artefact that is created for a purpose. However, a logically prior question concerns why it is that I think of myself as an artefact, as a created being. Only if I think of myself as a created being does it make sense for me to ask about the purpose for which I am created, the 'Why am I here?' question.

Lewis presented his explanation for why I think of myself as a created entity in terms of the fact that I can and do reason. 'The problem is whether you or I can be ... a self-existent Reason'.[141] '[E]ither I am self-existent (a belief which no one can accept) *or* I am a colony of some Thought or Will that are self-existent'.[142] Lewis believed I cannot seriously believe I am a self-existent being. But what is a self-existent being? Lewis answered this question in the following way:

> This question [whether you are or I am a self-existent Reason] almost answers itself the moment we remember what existence 'on one's own' means. It means that kind of existence which Naturalists attribute to 'the whole show' and Supernaturalists attribute to God. For instance, what exists on its own must have existed from all eternity ... It must also exist incessantly: that is, it cannot cease to exist and then begin again... Now it is clear that my Reason has grown up gradually since my birth and is interrupted for several hours each night. I therefore cannot be that eternal self-existent Reason which neither slumbers nor sleeps. Yet if any thought is valid, such a Reason must exist and must be the source of my own imperfect and intermittent rationality. Human minds, then, are not the only supernatural entities that exist. They do not come from nowhere. Each has come into Nature from Supernature: each has its tap-root in an eternal, self-existent, rational Being, whom we call God.[143]

Lewis made additional comments about a self-existent being a few paragraphs later:

---

[140] C. S. Lewis, *A Preface to Paradise Lost* (Oxford University Press, 1942), 1.
[141] Lewis, *Miracles*, 42.   [142] Lewis, 'Bulverism', 276.   [143] Lewis, *Miracles*, 42–3.

> In a pond whose surface was completely covered with scum and floating vegetation, there might be a few water-lilies. And you might of course be interested in them for their beauty. But you might also be interested in them because from their structure you could deduce that they had stalks underneath which went down to roots in the bottom. The Naturalist thinks that the pond (Nature – the great event in space and time) is of an indefinite depth – that there is nothing but water however far you go down. My claim is that some of the things on the surface (i.e., in our experience) show the contrary. These things (rational minds [souls]) reveal, on inspection, that they at least are not floating but attached by stalks to the bottom. Therefore the pond has a bottom. It is not pond, pond for ever. Go deep enough and you will come to something that is not pond – to mud and earth and then to rock and finally the whole bulk of Earth and the subterranean fire.[144]

While it is fairly clear what Lewis was getting at when he talked about a self-existent being, a few clarifying comments are warranted. Though naturalists might, as Lewis wrote, attribute self-existence to 'the whole show', and super-naturalists attribute self-existence to God, these attributions do not provide much help with understanding what 'self-existence' means. To tell the reader that a self-existent being must have existed from all eternity supplies a bit more information because it communicates the idea that a self-existent being has never not existed. But never to have come into existence, though necessary, is not sufficient for self-existence. To see why, it is helpful to contrast the idea of a self-existent being with that of a contingent being, which is a being that, though it exists, might not have existed. And it might not have existed, even if there were never a first moment at which it came into existence. As the philosopher Richard Taylor made clear,

> the concept of creation ... is often misunderstood, particularly by those whose thinking has been influenced by Christian ideas. People tend to think that creation – for example, the creation of the world by God – *means* creation *in time*, from which it of course logically follows that if the world had no beginning in time, then it cannot be the creation of God. This, however, is erroneous, for creation means essentially *dependence*, even in Christian theology. If one thing is the creation of another, then it depends for its existence on that other, and this is perfectly consistent with saying that both are eternal, that neither ever came into being, and hence, that neither was ever created at any point of time.[145]

According to Taylor, while a self-existent being has existed from all eternity, a being that has existed from all eternity might or might not be self-existent. If a being that has existed from all eternity is a dependent being, then it is not self-existent but is

---
[144] Lewis, *Miracles*, 45.
[145] Richard Taylor, *Metaphysics*, 4th ed. (Prentice-Hall, 1992), 103–4.

a contingent being that depends *at every moment that it exists*, however long that is, on the existence of a self-existent being. Lewis wrote about our relationship with God that 'I presume that only God's attention keeps me (or anything else) in existence at all'.[146] 'He makes, we are made: He is original, we derivative. But at the same time, and for the same reason, the intimacy between God and even the meanest creature is closer than any that creatures can attain with one another. Our life [existence] is, at every moment, supplied by Him.'[147]

The idea that at every moment our existence is supplied by God is essentially the idea that Lewis sought to communicate when he wrote about water-lilies on the surface of a pond having stalks that go down through the water to subterranean fire. The water-lilies are contingent beings that causally depend at every moment that they exist on the self-existent subterranean fire. The dependency relation involves simultaneous causality, and there cannot be pond, pond *ad infinitum* in terms of depth. At some point, there must be a self-existent bottom. Lewis gave another illustration of the idea of simultaneous causal dependency in terms of a supportive relation between books:

> Imagine two books lying on a table one on top of the other. Obviously the bottom book is keeping the other one up – supporting it. It is because of the underneath book that the top one is resting, say, two inches from the surface of the table instead of touching the table. Let us call the underneath book A and the top one B. The position of A is causing the position of B... Now let us imagine... that both books have been in that position for ever and ever. In that case B's position would always have been resulting from A's position. But all the same, A's position would not have existed before B's position. In other words the result does not come *after* the cause.[148]

In this example, the books stand in the same spatial relation for ever and ever, yet one of the books depends for its position on the causal support of the other book. Lewis might have tweaked this example slightly to make it accord with his example of the water-lilies. In this slightly altered case, a contingent being, represented by a book, ultimately depends causally for its existence on a self-existent being, represented by the table. While as a matter of fact in our world the books and table exist prior to entering into the supportive causal relation between them, the point Lewis would be making would be that the existence of the books is ultimately explained in terms of the self-existent being (the table) on whose existence they causally depend. The self-existent being causes the existence of the books at every moment of their existence for however long they exist. As Lewis wrote, a created being is 'an essentially dependent being whose

---

[146] Lewis, *Letters to Malcolm*, 20. [147] Lewis, *The Problem of Pain*, 33.
[148] Lewis, *Mere Christianity*, 172.

principle of existence lies not in itself but in another'.[149] Hence, 'Man', as a created being, 'is to be understood only in his relation to God'.[150] In sum, Lewis maintained that it is 'from the mere fact of our own existence [that] we already know to some extent which [statements about God] are [true and] which [are false]. We know that He invents, acts, creates'.[151] From our knowledge that we lack self-existence, we know that there is a self-existent being who creates us, a being to which we ascribe the name 'God'.

It is important to make explicit that in inferring the existence of an independent or self-existent being from the existence of himself as a dependent being, Lewis is reasoning from his existence as a dependent *soul*. He is not reasoning from the existence of his material body. Lewis thought that the existence of his material body was causally explained in terms of the sexual activity of his parents and the formation of a new body and the addition of parts to it over time. Lewis also believed that the ultimate constituents of the material world were themselves dependent beings and causally created and sustained in existence by a self-existent being, but the existence and nature of the material world is not the subject of his argument for the existence of a self-existent being.

So, Lewis maintained that the self-existent being causally explains the existence of a contingent being. Does the self-existent being's existence have an explanation? Or is it a brute fact without explanation, one which is a 'completely opaque *datum*'[152] 'with no discoverable rhyme or reason'?[153] It is highly doubtful Lewis believed God's self-existence is brute in this sense. Lewis was, like all of us, someone who was 'influenced by some innate sense of the fitness of things'.[154] He was, like all of us, someone who sought to understand the intelligibility located in the nature of things.[155] For example, in arguing for God's existence as the enforcer of justice in the universe he wrote the following:

> Thus in the very act of trying to prove that God did not exist – in other words, that the whole of reality was senseless – I found I was forced to assume that one part of reality – namely my idea of justice – was full of sense. Consequently atheism turns out to be too simple. If the whole universe has no meaning, we should never have found out that it has no meaning [to know

---

[149] Lewis, *The Problem of Pain*, 69.   [150] Lewis, *The Problem of Pain*, 142.
[151] Lewis, *Miracles*, 141–2.   [152] Lewis, *Letters to Malcolm*, 103.   [153] Lewis, *Miracles*, 88.
[154] Lewis, *Miracles*, 166.
[155] Lewis wrote that 'the sciences are always pushing further back the realm of mere "brute fact." But no scientist, I suppose, believes that the process could ever reach completion. At the very least, there must always remain the utterly "brute" fact ... that a universe – or, rather, *this* universe with its determinate character – exists'. (Lewis, *Letters to Malcolm*, 103–4). But Lewis insisted a scientist is also a human being, and as a human being the scientist believes there are no brute facts.

something does not make sense one must presuppose a backdrop of what would make sense].[156]

This quote comes from the first section of *Mere Christianity* entitled 'Right and Wrong as a Clue to the Meaning of the Universe', which in light of the quotation just cited can reasonably be translated 'Right and Wrong as a Clue to the Universe's Making Sense/Being Intelligible'. Elsewhere, Lewis described God as the self-existent being 'which has Its principle of being [the explanation of its existence] in Itself'.[157] And, 'if we fully understood *what* God is we should see that there is no question *whether* He is. It would always have been impossible that He should not exist'.[158]

What explains the existence of the self-existent being? So far as I know, Lewis never explicitly answered this question. The best that I can do at this point is describe the logical alternatives and reasonably hypothesize what Lewis would have said about them.

The logical alternatives are two. The first is that God's existence is logically necessary in the sense that God's existence is a part of His nature, so that 'God does not exist' is a logical contradiction, just as being unmarried is part of the nature of bachelorhood so that 'It is false that a bachelor is unmarried' is a logical contradiction. On this alternative, to deny that God exists or that a bachelor is unmarried expresses an absurdity.

The second alternative is that God's existence is metaphysically necessary in the sense that while God's existence is not part of His nature and, therefore, it is not absurd to deny God's existence, it is nevertheless the case that 'God does not exist' is necessarily false. As I discussed in the previous section, Lewis believed it is metaphysically necessary that an experience of pleasure is intrinsically good. He believed that while the nature of pleasure implies its intrinsic goodness, it is not absurd to affirm 'Pleasure is not intrinsically good' because the goodness of pleasure, though implied by the nature of pleasure, is not a part of that nature. Though 'Pleasure is not intrinsically good' is not a logical contradiction, it is necessarily false.

Issues concerning self-existence and kinds of necessity are complicated, but it is plausible to think that Lewis, because he tried to make ultimate sense of things on the basis of his belief that things are ultimately intelligible, was convinced that the distinction between a logically and metaphysically necessary being is real and that God is either one or the other. Support for this position is twofold.

---

[156] Lewis, *Mere Christianity*, 38–9.   [157] Lewis, *The Problem of Pain*, 33.
[158] Lewis, *Miracles*, 141.

First, when Lewis discussed whether God is ultimately righteous and loving, he wrote that a man is not logically compelled to affirm that God has these properties: 'At every stage of religious development man may rebel, if not without violence to his own nature, yet without absurdity'.[159] In other words, Lewis believed a man can do that which, though contrary to his nature, is not logically absurd (which is in keeping with the point that denying pleasure's goodness is contrary to its nature but not logically absurd), which suggests Lewis thought the distinction between metaphysical and logical necessity is real.

Second, support for the view that Lewis believed God's existence is either logically or metaphysically necessary is provided through a consideration of why he thought he was not a self-existent but a contingent being. Presumably, Lewis believed that his existence was neither logically nor metaphysically necessary because 'C. S. Lewis does not exist' is neither logically contradictory nor necessarily false, which implies he believed his existence was logically and metaphysically contingent. Why not think Lewis believed his own existence was brute and inexplicable? He believed it would make no sense to maintain that he was a contingent being whose existence had no explanation. Had he believed his own existence was brute, he would have believed not only that he was neither a logically nor a metaphysically necessary being but also that there was no explanation for his existence. As I have already quoted, Lewis believed 'Human minds', because they are contingent, 'do not come from nowhere',[160] which is to say they do not come from nothing without a cause. In short, given Lewis thought that his existence was both logically and metaphysically contingent and yet had a causal explanation, it is reasonable to conclude that he also thought God's existence had an explanation.[161] Given that the explanation for God's existence could not be causal in nature because God is self-existent, Lewis would have concluded that God's existence must be either logically or metaphysically necessary.

I began this section with a quote from Lewis about corkscrews and cathedrals as artefacts created for purposes, where a purpose is a kind of explanation which philosophers refer to as a teleological explanation. While Lewis believed his existence had a causal explanation in terms of God as a necessary being, he believed this causal explanation was not a complete explanation of his existence. Lewis seems non-inferentially to have believed that God caused him to

---

[159] Lewis, *The Problem of Pain*, 14.   [160] Lewis, *Miracles*, 43.
[161] I am assuming that Lewis believed there was no principled way of justifiably affirming that reality, in terms of his own existence, had to make sense, but reality, in terms of the existence of God, did not. That is, Lewis believed it would have been completely arbitrary, and, thus, have made no sense, to demand affirmation of the former but not the latter.

exist for a purpose, because without such a purpose his existence would not have ultimately made sense. What Lewis thought about this purpose is the subject of the next section.

Because Lewis believed his existence must have a purpose in order for it to be fully intelligible, one might wonder whether Lewis also believed God's existence must have a purpose in order to be completely intelligible. I think there is good reason to maintain that Lewis thought God's existence was purposeless (without a purpose) because he believed the idea of an entity's having a purpose was essentially linked to its being an artefact and, thus, caused to exist. Given that God is a necessary being and as such never came into existence, His existence could not have a teleological explanation.

In the end, it is because we lack an understanding of what explains the logical or metaphysical necessity of God's existence that Lewis maintained God 'is the opaque centre of all existences'.[162] Of 'the self-existing Being … no man … can … conceive what He is in and for Himself'.[163] Generally, 'there is something in our very mode of thought which makes it inevitable that we should always be baffled by actual existence, *whatever* character actual existence may have'.[164]

3.3 Faith-A and Faith-B

Lewis inferred belief in God's existence from his non-inferential belief that he is a contingent soul. He considered inferential belief in God's existence as 'a settled intellectual assent' and termed this assent 'Faith-A'.[165] It is important to make two points here concerning Faith-A.

First, Lewis stated that as a rule people, when they say they believe something, convey the idea that they are to some degree less than certain about the truth of what they believe.[166] However, he held that there are two notable exceptions to this rule. One is when a person says 'I don't believe it'. This assertion might well imply a degree of certitude that in terms of subjective conviction is like that had by an individual when he says that he knows something. For example, if a materialist hears of a report of a miracle, he will

---

[162] Lewis, *Miracles*, 141.
[163] Lewis, *The Problem of Pain*, 159. Though no man can conceive of what God is in and for Himself, God can. Lewis wrote that 'the property of a self-existent being is that it can [directly] understand its own existence. The quality of a created being is that it just finds itself existing, it knows not how nor why [but must infer knowledge of these things]'. *A Preface to Paradise Lost*, 97.
[164] C. S. Lewis, 'Dogma and the Universe', in *God in the Dock*, ed. Walter Hooper (Eerdmans, [1943] in 1970), 40.
[165] Lewis, 'Is Theism Important?', 172–3.
[166] C. S. Lewis, 'On Obstinacy in Belief', in *The World's Last Night and Other Essays*, ed. Walter Hooper (Harcourt, [1955] in 1987), 14–15.

reply 'I don't believe it', where his certitude, though likely lacking the support of a formal demonstration of the impossibility of miracles, is complete. The second exception to the rule is when a person says 'I believe that God exists'. Here, the believer might or might not have at hand what he takes to be a formal demonstration of God's existence. Regardless, his belief that God exists psychologically excludes all doubt, even though there is logical space for dispute. Lewis thought that the belief that God exists is not unlike the belief in the existence of the material world or other souls 'inside' human bodies. All ordinary people believe in these things, though 'far in excess of [their] strongest arguments',[167] or without any argument whatsoever.

Second, inferential assent or belief in God in the sense of Faith-A is a necessary condition of belief as trust or confidence in the God of Faith-A. Lewis termed belief as trust or confidence 'Faith-B'.[168] 'The object of [Faith-B] is ... the *ens entium* [being of beings] of the philosophers'.[169] With Faith-B we have moved from the logic of speculative thought that is involved in Faith-A to the logic of personal relations.[170]

Most generally then, Lewis conceived of the strands of any developed religion (awe of the numinous, morality, and the numinous as the guardian of morality) being converted or transformed into Faith-B via an argument for belief in the existence of God. However, he was well aware that arguments other than that from the soul's contingency have been given for belief in the existence of the God of Faith-A. He commented that

> [n]early everyone I know who has embraced Christianity [an instance of Faith-B] in adult life has been influenced by what seemed to him to be at least probable arguments for Theism... Even acceptance of tradition implies an argument which sometimes becomes explicit in the form 'I reckon all those wise men wouldn't have believed in it if it weren't true'.[171]

In the next section, I present a brief summary of what Lewis had to say about two traditional arguments for belief in the existence of the God of Faith-A.

3.4 The Material World and Inferential Belief that God Exists

Among philosophers, an argument from the existence of the material world as a contingent being to the existence of a necessary being is standardly referred to as a cosmological argument. It is an argument from effect to cause. Strictly speaking, Lewis's argument from the soul's contingency to the existence of a necessary being is not a cosmological argument. This is because even though

---

[167] Lewis, 'On Obstinacy in Belief', 16.   [168] Lewis, 'Is Theism Important?', 172–3.
[169] Lewis, 'Is Theism Important?', 175.   [170] Lewis, 'On Obstinacy in Belief', 30.
[171] Lewis, 'Is Theism Important?', 173.

it is an argument from effect to cause, it does not move from the existence of the material cosmos as a contingent being to the existence of a necessary being. Hence, it is best to think of Lewis's causal argument as a species of a genus of causal arguments for the existence of a necessary being.

Did Lewis find a cosmological argument convincing? He wrote to his friend Dom Bede Griffiths that he did not: '[T]he Cosmological argument is, for some people at some times, ineffective. It has always been for me'.[172] While he was aware of the 'big bang' theory about the universe's origin which supports the view that '[t]he universe had a beginning, and will have an end', he cautioned that '[w]e should not lean too heavily on this [theory], for scientific theories change'.[173]

Moreover, Lewis believed that '[i]n popular thought ... the origin of the universe has counted (I think) for less than its character – its immense size and apparent indifference, if not hostility, to human life'.[174] About the character of space, Lewis wrote that 'we certainly perceive it as three-dimensional, and to three-dimensional space we can conceive no boundaries. By the very forms of our perception, therefore, we must feel as if we lived somewhere in infinite space'.[175] But while we as individuals feel dwarfed by the size of the universe and, perhaps, conclude that we lack any value, Lewis insisted our size relative to that of the universe has nothing to do with whether we as individual human beings have any value:

> If size and value had any real connexion, small differences in size would accompany small differences in value as surely as large differences in size accompany large differences in value. But no sane man could suppose this is so. I don't think the taller man *slightly* more valuable than the shorter one. I don't allow a slight superiority [in value] to trees over men, and then neglect it because it is too small to bother about. I perceive, as long as I am dealing with small differences of size, that they have no connexion with value whatsoever. I therefore conclude that the importance attached to the great differences of size is an affair, not of reason but of emotion – of that peculiar emotion which superiorities in size produce only after a certain point of absolute size has been reached.[176]

Another consideration for belief in the existence of God is provided by the apparent purpose found in objects in the material world.[177] Given this appearance of design, individuals infer the existence of a designer. One of the most widely discussed teleological arguments was that of the eighteenth-century

---

[172] Lewis, *The Collected Letters, Volume III*, 195.   [173] Lewis, 'Dogma and the Universe', 39.
[174] Lewis, 'Dogma and the Universe', 39.   [175] Lewis, 'Dogma and the Universe', 40.
[176] Lewis, 'Dogma and the Universe', 41.
[177] Even the atheist Richard Dawkins insists upon the 'appearance of design' in nature (Richard Dawkins, *The Blind Watchmaker* (Norton, 1987), 21).

English divine William Paley. Paley maintained that the organized complexity of the human eye required a designer with the requisite intelligence to produce it.[178]

Did Lewis find a teleological argument convincing? He wrote that he did not. What impressed him more about the external world was the apparent disteleology of pain and suffering in it. When he explained as a theist in 1940 why he had been an atheist a few years earlier, he wrote the following:

> Look at the universe we live in... [W]hat is it like while it lasts? It is so arranged that all the forms of it can live only by preying upon one another. In the lower forms this process entails only death, but in the higher there appears a new quality called consciousness which enables it to be attended with pain. The creatures cause pain by being born, and live by inflicting pain, and in pain they mostly die. In the most complex of all the creatures, Man, yet another quality appears, which we call reason, whereby he is enabled to foresee his own pain which henceforth is preceded with acute mental suffering, and to foresee his own death while keenly desiring permanence. It also enables men by a hundred ingenious contrivances to inflict a great deal more pain than they otherwise could have done on one another and on the irrational creatures.[179]

What conclusion might one reasonably infer from this 'evidence'? Lewis answered,

> If you ask me to believe that this is the work of a benevolent and omnipotent spirit, I reply that all the evidence points in the opposite direction. Either there is no spirit behind the universe, or else a spirit indifferent to good and evil, or else an evil spirit... The direct inference from black to white, from evil flower to virtuous root, from senseless work to a workman infinitely wise, staggers belief. The spectacle of the universe as revealed by experience can never have been the ground of religion: it must always have been something in spite of which religion, acquired from a different source, was held.[180]

In a letter to a friend in 1946, Lewis said, 'I still think the argument from design the weakest possible ground for Theism [a belief that God exists], and what may be called the argument from un-design the strongest for Atheism'.[181]

Lewis thought that what people conclude about the reality of design in the external world is a reflection of what they think about themselves. If they believe they are souls which are artefacts created by a designer for a purpose, then they will not dismiss the appearances of design in the external world as illusory. And they will conclude that the evils they see in

---

[178] William Paley, 'The Watch and the Watchmaker', in *Philosophy of Religion: An Anthology*, ed. Louis P. Pojman (Wadsworth, [1802] in 1987), 29–31.
[179] Lewis, *The Problem of Pain*, 1–2.   [180] Lewis, *The Problem of Pain*, 3–4.
[181] Lewis, *The Collected Letters, Volume II*, 747.

the external world are compatible with the moral goodness of the designer: '[I]f God is good (and I think we have grounds for saying that he is) then the appearance of divine cruelty in the animal world must be a false appearance'.[182] If they believe they are material entities which are not created for a purpose, then they will regard the appearances of design in the external world as illusory: 'In so far as natural science can give a satisfactory account of man as a purely biological entity, it excludes the soul and ... scientists who are most, or most nearly, concerned with man himself are the most anti-religious'.[183] And they will conclude that the evils they believe they see in the external world, provided they do not deny their reality, are the effects of an ultimately blind and careless universe.

Most generally, Lewis believed nature as a whole is a mixed bag. It has instances of design and of 'terror, gloom, jocundity, cruelty, lust, innocence, [and] purity'.[184] 'If you take nature as a teacher she will teach you exactly the lessons you had already decided to learn; this is only another way of saying that nature does not teach... We must learn our theology or philosophy elsewhere'.[185] A man can clothe his belief, whether in God or nature as a material causal system without purpose, with what he finds in nature. Thus, concluded Lewis, not only does nature as a whole not teach the existence of a designer who is morally good, but also it does not teach that

> there exists a God of glory and of infinite majesty. I had to learn that in other ways. But nature gave the word *glory* a meaning for me... Nature cannot ... answer theological questions ... Our real journey to God involves constantly turning our backs on her; passing from the dawn-lit fields into some pokey little church ...'[186]

3.5 From Theism to Life's Purpose and Christianity

Lewis believed we are contingent beings who are continuously causally dependent on God for our existence. But why does God cause us to exist? For what purpose? And why does Lewis think it is reasonable for a theist to be a Christian? These are the subjects of the next section.

---

[182] C. S. Lewis, 'The Pains of Animals', in *God in the Dock*, ed. Walter Hooper (Eerdmans, [1950] in 1970), 167–8.
[183] Lewis, 'Religion without Dogma?', 135. Dawkins, as a naturalist, concludes the appearance of design in objects in the natural world is illusory. See *The Blind Watchmaker*, 1987.
[184] Lewis, *The Four Loves*, 19.   [185] Lewis, *The Four Loves*, 19.
[186] Lewis, *The Four Loves*, 20, 21–2.

4 Life's End and Christianity

4.1 The Purpose of Life

For Lewis, the belief that God exists is inferred from knowledge of the contingent nature of the self. Because Lewis believed we are contingent souls created by God, he viewed us as artefacts which are made by an Artificer for an end or purpose. While many people naturally think it is good news that there is a purpose of life, others think it is bad news. For example, the philosopher Kurt Baier claimed the idea that there is a purpose of life is demeaning or degrading:

> To attribute to a human being a purpose in [the sense of the purpose of an artefact] is not neutral, let alone complimentary: it is offensive. It is degrading for a man to be regarded as merely serving a purpose. If, at a garden party, I ask a man in livery, 'What is your purpose?' I am insulting him. I might as well have asked, 'What are you *for*?' Such questions reduce him to the level of a gadget, a domestic animal, or perhaps a slave. I imply that *we* allot to *him* the tasks, the goals, the aims which he is to pursue; that *his* wishes and desires and aspirations and purposes are to count for little or nothing.[187]

Given Lewis thought that pain is intrinsically evil, it is plausible to conclude he would have agreed with Baier that a purpose of life according to which our end is to suffer would be demeaning. However, Lewis would have pointed out that it is false to claim that having a purpose of life is essentially degrading. Whether it is degrading depends upon what the purpose is. Given that Lewis believed pleasure is intrinsically good, he believed the purpose of life might be anything but demeaning. If we are created for the purpose of being perfectly, completely, infinitely, eternally, or blessedly happy, then the purpose of life is ennobling. Here, there is no need to conjecture about what Lewis believed. In *The Great Divorce*, a book about a fantastical bus trip to the outer reaches of heaven, one of the spectral visitors says 'I wish I'd never been born ... What *are* we born for?', to which a heavenly spirit answers, 'For infinite happiness'.[188] In 1933, not long after his affirmation of Christianity, Lewis wrote to his friend Arthur Greeves that 'God not only understands but *shares* the desire ... for complete and ecstatic happiness. He made me for no other purpose than to enjoy it'.[189] And during World War II, Lewis wrote that

> I provisionally define Agapë as 'steadily remembering that inside the Gestapo-man there is a thing [which] says I and Me just as you do, which

---

[187] Kurt Baier, 'The Meaning of Life', in *The Meaning of Life*, 2nd ed., ed. E. D. Klemke (Oxford University Press, 2000), 120.
[188] Lewis, *The Great Divorce*, 61. [189] Lewis, *The Collected Letters, Volume II*, 123.

has just the same grounds (neither more nor less) as your "Me" for being distinguished from all its sins however numerous, which, like you, was made by God for eternal happiness'.[190]

Lewis wrote elsewhere that infinite, complete, or ecstatic happiness is the life of the blessed, and he stated that we must suppose 'the life of the blessed to be an end in itself, indeed The End'.[191] He maintained that a Christian 'believes that men are going to live forever, [and] that they were created by God and so built that they can find their true and lasting happiness only by being united to God'.[192] When he referred in a letter to the Protestant Westminster Catechism, he stressed that 'Man was created to "glorify God and *enjoy* Him forever"'.[193]

It is important to make clear that Lewis was not out of step with the Christian tradition in his understanding of the purpose of life as perfect happiness. In the early Middle Ages, Saint Augustine (354–430) wrote that '[w]e wish to be happy, do we not? ... Everyone who possesses what he wants is happy ... Therefore ... whoever possesses God is happy'.[194] Not too long after Augustine, Boethius (480–524) wrote *The Consolation of Philosophy* in which his interlocutor Lady Philosophy reminded him that

> [t]he whole concern of men, which the effort of a multitude of pursuits keeps busy, moves by different roads, yet strives to arrive at one and the same end, that of happiness... In all of these things it is obviously happiness alone that is desired; for whatever a man seeks above all else, that he reckons the highest good. But we have defined the highest good as happiness; wherefore each man judges that state to be happy which he desires above all others... And you also, earthly creatures that you are, have some image, though hazy, in your dreams of your beginning; you see, though with a far from clear imagination yet with some idea, that true end of your happiness. Your natural inclinations draw you towards that end, to the true good.[195]

And a few centuries later, Saint Anselm (1033–1109) affirmed the idea that God created us for the purpose that we be completely happy: 'It ought not to be doubted that the nature of rational beings was created by God ... Man, being rational by nature, was created ... to the end that, through rejoicing in God, he might be blessedly happy... God ... [made man] for the purpose of eternal happiness'.[196]

---

[190] Lewis, *The Collected Letters, Volume II*, 409.   [191] Lewis, *Letters to Malcolm*, 92.
[192] Lewis, 'Man or Rabbit?', 109.   [193] Lewis, *The Collected Letters, Volume III*, 856.
[194] St. Augustine, 'The Happy Life', in *Happiness: Classic and Contemporary Readings*, ed. Steven M. Cahn and Christine Vitrano (Oxford University Press, 2008), 52–3.
[195] Boethius, *The Consolation of Philosophy*, trans. S. J. Tester (Harvard University Press, 1973), 233, 235, 241.
[196] St. Anselm, *Anselm of Canterbury: The Major Works*, ed. Brian Davies and G. R. Evans (Oxford University Press, 1998), 315–16.

Thomas Aquinas (1224/25–1274) agreed with Augustine, Boethius, and Anselm. According to Saint Thomas, 'the ultimate end of man ... is called felicity or happiness, because this is what every intellectual substance desires as an ultimate end, and for its own sake alone' (1975, 102). Because 'all creatures ... are ordered to God as to an ultimate end',[197] and 'the highest good for man ... is felicity',[198] it follows that 'man's ultimate felicity consists only in the contemplation of God'.[199] John Calvin (1509–1564) also believed we were created for the purpose that we be perfectly happy. According to him, in order that God 'may encourage us in every way, he promises present blessings, as well as eternal felicity, to the obedience of those who shall have kept his commands'.[200] Indeed, because the 'holy patriarchs expected a happy life from the hand of God (and it is indubitable that they did), they viewed and contemplated a different happiness from that of a terrestrial life'.[201] And, wrote Calvin, '[h]e who confesses that there is nothing solid or stable on the earth, and yet firmly retains his hope in God, undoubtedly contemplates a happiness reserved for him elsewhere'.[202]

While Lewis's view of the purpose of life is unremarkable in terms of the Christian tradition, it is noteworthy in terms of his belief that happiness consists of experiences of pleasure. Christian philosophers and theologians such as Thomas Aquinas in the eudaimonist tradition identified happiness with the contemplation of God.[203] Though Lewis did not repudiate the idea of the contemplation of God, he believed that if[204] the contemplation of God is involved in perfect happiness, it is not happiness itself but its source.

What about the purposes of things other than a human person? What about the purpose of the spiral nebulae? Lewis wrote, 'I have not the faintest idea why [God] made them; on the whole, I think it would be rather surprising if I had'.[205] And he added that Christianity does not provide such knowledge:

---

[197] St. Thomas Aquinas, *Summa Contra Gentiles: Book Three*, trans. Vernon J. Bourke (University of Notre Dame Press, 1975), 97.
[198] Aquinas, *Summa Contra Gentiles*, 113.   [199] Aquinas, *Summa Contra Gentiles*, 125.
[200] John Calvin, *The Institutes of the Christian Religion*, trans. Henry Beveridge (Hendrickson, 2008), II. 8. 4.
[201] Calvin, *The Institutes of the Christian Religion*, II. 10. 13.
[202] Calvin, *The Institutes of the Christian Religion*, II. 10. 15.
[203] Stewart Goetz, *A Philosophical Walking Tour with C. S. Lewis: Why It Did Not Include Rome* (Bloomsbury, 2015).
[204] Lewis was inclined to be noncommittal about the sources of pleasure in heaven because they have 'never actually been embodied in any thought, or image, or emotion' (Lewis, *The Problem of Pain*, 152–3). In the 'Christian picture of the universe ... [a] future state and orders of superhuman creatures are held to exist, but only the slightest hints of their nature are offered' ('Is Theology Poetry?', 118).
[205] Lewis, 'Dogma and the Universe', 42.

> Christianity is not wedded to an anthropocentric view of the universe as a whole... There are few places in literature where we are more sternly warned against making man the measure of all things than in the Book of Job: 'Canst thou draw out leviathan with an hook? Will he make a covenant with thee? wilt thou take him for a servant? Shall not one be cast down even at the sight of him? ... It is, of course, the essence of Christianity that God loves man and for his sake became man and died. But that does not prove that man is the sole end of nature... We are in no position to draw up maps of God's psychology, and prescribe limits to His interests... It is to be expected that His creation should be, in the main, unintelligible to us... [R]evelation appears to me to be ... addressed ... not to the spirit of inquiry in man for the gratification of his liberal curiosity.[206]

Lewis believed not only that we do not know the purpose of the starry expanses, but also we do not know the purpose of the beasts. 'We know neither why they were made nor what they are'.[207] While we have epistemic access to the purpose for which we are created, we lack such access to the purposes of other divine artefacts.

4.2 The Divine Command Theory of Morality

While Lewis believed we do not know why God chose to create the celestial orbs and the earthly beasts, he held that God did choose to make them. But Lewis maintained not everything is the result of a choice of God. It is because Lewis believed pleasure is intrinsically good and pain is intrinsically evil, which implies that their values could not be the result of anyone's choice, that he rejected the divine-command theory of morality according to which murder, lying, adultery, and so on are morally wrong or unjust because God chose (commanded) that they be so. Lewis understood that once God created souls that can experience pleasure and pain, moral principles followed logically from the non-moral qualitative natures of pleasure and pain as intrinsically good and intrinsically evil respectively. For example, Lewis thought that taking the life of someone else for no good reason (i.e., committing murder) is unjust because it deprives the victim of the opportunity in this life to experience the pleasure for which he was created. And depriving a person for no good reason of the truth that he needs to protect himself from harm and enjoy the happiness for which he is created is similarly unjust.

The question of whether, say, lying is morally wrong because God says it is morally wrong was posed by Plato almost twenty-four hundred years ago in what is now known as Euthyphro's Dilemma. In his dialogue, *Euthyphro*, a question is raised whether an action is pious because the gods say it is pious

---

[206] Lewis, 'Dogma and the Universe', 42–3. [207] Lewis, *The Problem of Pain*, 133.

or whether the gods say that action is pious because it is pious. If we substitute the idea of good, right, or just for that of piety, we can ask whether an action is morally good, right, or just because God says it is morally so or whether God says it is morally good, right, or just because it is so. Lewis made clear that he sided with the alternative that God says an action is morally just because it is morally just. Lewis believed that embracing the other alternative, that an action is morally just because God says it is morally just, leads to a problem of arbitrariness where an action such as murder could be morally just because God says it is. Lewis wrote that morality is an expression of what God necessarily is, which is morally good or righteous, because God's choice or will is necessarily determined by what He perceives or understands is morally good or just:

> With Hooker, and against Dr Johnson, I emphatically embrace the first alternative [God says an action is good because it is good]. The second [an action is good because God says it is good] might lead to the abominable conclusion ... that charity is good only because God arbitrarily commanded it – that He might equally well have commanded us to hate Him and one another and that hatred would then have been right... God's will is determined by His wisdom which always perceives, and His goodness which always embraces, the intrinsically good.[208]
>
> If I had any hesitation in saying that God 'made' the *Tao* [the moral law] it [would] only be because that might suggest that it was an arbitrary creation ... : whereas I believe it to be the necessary expression, in terms of temporal existence, of what God by His own righteous nature necessarily is. One [could] indeed say of it *genitum, non factum* [begotten, not made]: for is not the *Tao* the Word Himself, considered from a particular point of view?[209]
>
> There were in the eighteenth century terrible theologians who held that 'God did not command certain things because they are right, but certain things are right because God commanded them'... Such a view of course makes God a mere arbitrary tyrant.[210]

4.3 The Argument from Desire

Lewis believed morality is a function of the nature of experiences of pleasure and pain. Given the nature of pleasure as intrinsically good, Lewis thought that, all else being equal, it is impossible not to desire that one's current experiences of pleasure continue indefinitely, and if one is not currently experiencing pleasure then that one come to do so. And because Lewis believed experiences

---

[208] Lewis, *The Problem of Pain*, 99.   [209] Lewis, *The Collected Letters, Volume III*, 1226–7.
[210] Lewis, *Reflections on the Psalms*, 61.

of pleasure constitute happiness, he believed one desired to experience everlasting happiness:

> [W]e remain conscious of a desire which no natural happiness will satisfy. But is there any reason to suppose that reality offers any satisfaction to it? 'Nor does the being hungry prove that we have bread'. But I think it may be urged that this misses the point. A man's physical hunger does not prove that man will get any bread; he may die of starvation on a raft in the Atlantic. But surely a man's hunger does prove that he comes of a race which repairs its body by eating and inhabits a world where eatable substances exist. In the same way, though I do not believe ... that my desire for Paradise proves that I shall enjoy it, I think it a pretty good indication that such a thing exists and that some men will. A man may love a woman and not win her; but it would be very odd if the phenomenon called 'falling in love' occurred in a sexless world.[211]

And:

> Creatures are not born with desires unless satisfaction for those desires exists. A baby feels hunger: well, there is such a thing as food. A duckling wants to swim: well, there is such a thing as water. Men feel sexual desire: well, there is such a thing as sex. If I find in myself a desire which no experience in this world can satisfy, the most probable explanation is that I was made for another world. If none of my earthly pleasures satisfy it, that does not prove that the universe is a fraud. Probably earthly pleasures were never meant to satisfy it, but only to arouse it, to suggest the real thing.[212]

Others who have written about Lewis's thoughts concerning religious belief have seen in the passages just quoted a rough attempt at an argument from what we desire to the existence of the afterlife and God.[213] John Beversluis understood the passages in this way and believed the argument fallacious:

> The phenomenon of hunger simply does not prove that man inhabits a world in which food exists. One might just as well claim that the fear that grips us when we walk through a dark graveyard proves that we have something to be afraid of. What proves that we inhabit a world in which food exists is the discovery that certain things are in fact 'eatable' and that they nourish and repair our bodies. The discovery of the existence of food comes not by way of an inference based on the inner state of hunger; it is, rather an empirical discovery.... Just as we cannot prove that we inhabit a world in which food exists simply on the ground that we get hungry, so we cannot prove that an infinite Object [perfect happiness] of desire exists simply on the ground that we desire it.[214]

---

[211] Lewis, 'The Weight of Glory', 32–3.   [212] Lewis, *Mere Christianity*, 136–7.
[213] See Alister McGrath, *The Intellectual World of C. S. Lewis* (Wiley-Blackwell, 2014), 105–28.
[214] John Beversluis, *C. S. Lewis and the Search for Rational Religion* (Eerdmans, 1985), 18–19.

Beversluis's response seems perfectly reasonable, if he has understood Lewis's thought correctly. But has he? Erik Wielenberg suggests we look for a different interpretation of Lewis's 'argument from desire'.[215] He believes Lewis was pointing out that if the desire for perfect happiness cannot be fulfilled, then the universe fails to make sense. This reading is suggested by Lewis's mention of the ideas of oddness and fraudulence for desires that cannot be satisfied. We are all too aware that the desire for perfect happiness is not fulfilled in this life. If there is no afterlife in which it can be fulfilled, then the universe is fraudulent in the sense that things ultimately do not fit together in the correct way. They are odd or out of sorts. They do not in the end make sense. Our existence is unreasonable or absurd.

Weston, the mad physicist in *Perelandra*, concludes 'reasoning ... has nothing to do with the real universe [and] reality is neither rational nor consistent', to which the philologist Ransom responds '[i]f ... this were true ... what would be the point of saying it?'[216] It makes no sense to defend the view that nothing real makes any sense. Wielenberg believes a naturalist can make sense of the desire for perfect happiness in evolutionary terms. By hypothesis, evolution selects for traits in organisms that are advantageous for survival and reproduction. Therefore, given we possess the desire for perfect happiness, we should seek to see if it can be understood as beneficial for survival and reproduction. The following is Wielenberg's suggestion for so understanding this desire:

> The first important fact is that one of the main effects of [the desire for perfect happiness] is that it prevents a person from deriving lasting contentment from earthly things. This fact is important because deriving lasting contentment from earthly things can be quite disadvantageous, evolutionarily speaking. Dissatisfaction can benefit us in the long run. This idea is evident in Ronald Dworkin's criticism of the use of psychotropic drugs as a 'treatment' for ordinary unhappiness ... Dworkin labels the happiness produced in this way 'Artificial Happiness' and observes that '[p]eople with Artificial Happiness don't feel the unhappiness they need to move forward with their lives'. To see the evolutionary drawbacks of lasting contentment, consider a male human who is perfectly content as long as his basic needs (food, shelter, and sex) are satisfied. Once such needs are satisfied, he will have no motivation whatsoever to acquire additional wealth, power, status, or success; indeed, he will have no motivation to do anything at all, other than perhaps ensure that his basic needs continue to be satisfied. Contrast this male with a second male who has the same basic drives but who *never* achieves lasting contentment ...

---

[215] Erik Wielenberg, *God and the Reach of Reason: C. S. Lewis, David Hume, and Bertrand Russell* (Cambridge University Press, 2008), 108–20.
[216] Lewis, *Perelandra*, 144.

Everything else being equal, the second male will likely do better than the first in the competition for limited resources... Evolutionarily speaking, a good strategy is never to be entirely satisfied with one's lot in life.[217]

In sum, '[b]y causing us to strive for the infinite, [the desire for perfect happiness] prevents us from being entirely satisfied by the finite, and in this way causes us to survive and reproduce more successfully than we otherwise would'.[218]

Given an understanding of Lewis's previous critique of naturalism, it is possible to raise several points that he likely would have made in response to Wielenberg's argument. First and foremost, it is reasonable to think that Lewis would have insisted that deriving lasting contentment (experiencing perfect happiness) from something is essentially not disadvantageous. Because he believed perfect happiness is intrinsically good, he would have insisted that anyone who experiences it would not be at all concerned with the fact that he did not need to compete for survival (by hypothesis, competing for survival is painful and, thus, could in principle have no place in perfect happiness). Indeed, he would have thought that anyone who experiences perfect happiness is thankful that he does not have to compete for anything.

Second, and again in light of his belief in the intrinsic goodness of perfect happiness, Lewis would have maintained that a person is interested in surviving only if he believes it is possible to be sufficiently happy: 'I care far more how humanity lives than how long. Progress, for me, means increasing goodness and happiness of individual lives. For the species, as for each man, mere longevity seems to me a contemptible ideal'.[219] In terms of perfect happiness which, by hypothesis, is everlasting, Lewis thought it is belief in the possibility of experiencing perfect happiness with its intrinsic goodness that explains the desire to survive. The concept of survival does no explanatory work on its own. In Lewis's view, Wielenberg's naturalistic evolutionary explanation of the desire for perfect happiness gets the explanatory story backwards.

Third, Lewis would have made clear that Wielenberg's evolutionary explanation of the desire for perfect happiness accords explanatory power to desire: the desire for perfect happiness explains survival events in the material world. Because desire is a mental event, Wielenberg, given his evolutionary explanation is naturalistic, illicitly includes a mental explanation of at least some material events.

Fourth, Lewis would likely have raised a question about whether Wielenberg's evolutionary explanation of the desire for perfect happiness

---

[217] Wielenberg, *God and the Reach of Reason*, 116–17.
[218] Wielenberg, *God and the Reach of Reason*, 117.   [219] Lewis, 'Is Progress Possible?', 311.

ultimately (in the end) makes sense. In order to clarify why Lewis would have believed this question is justified, he would have needed to distinguish between consideration of a desire in terms of its causal connections and consideration of a desire in terms of its fulfilment.

Wielenberg is seeking to make sense of the desire for perfect happiness in terms of how it relates causally to other events such as the eating of food, the securing of shelter, survival, and sexual reproduction. Lewis likely would have suggested that even if we disregard the first three points made in response on his behalf to Wielenberg's argument and concede that Wielenberg has made sense of the desire for perfect happiness in terms of its causal relations, Wielenberg has not made sense of this desire in terms of the fulfilment of its content. The desire for perfect happiness is impossible to fulfil because naturalism implies the non-existence of an afterlife. Thus, the universe is ultimately absurd. Indeed, Wielenberg acknowledges that 'there is something "out of kilter" about the universe in that it is part of human nature to desire something that does not exist'.[220] He adds, 'I do not see that the mere fact that a view ... implies that the world is absurd ... constitutes a reason for thinking that the view in question is false'.[221]

Lewis would have agreed with Wielenberg that the fact that a view implies the world is absurd in some way does not falsify the view, provided the absurdity is *not ultimate* in nature. Lewis recognized that the world is all too often absurd non-ultimately (in the short run) in so far as our desire for happiness in the here and now goes unfulfilled. However, Wielenberg's view makes sense of the desire for perfect happiness at the expense of the impossibility of its ever being fulfilled. The absurdity is ultimate in nature. Lewis would have stressed that just as we are perfectionists in our desire for happiness (we desire that our happiness be perfect in nature), so also we are perfectionists in our desire to make sense of things (we desire that things make perfect sense). He believed that in so far as theism contains no absurdity regarding fulfilment of the desire for perfect happiness, it does a better job of making ultimate sense of things.

Of course, to experience perfect happiness beyond this world requires the survival of the self. Lewis thought this was not metaphysically problematic because each of us is a soul that God keeps in existence in this world and the afterlife. Naturalists deny the existence of the soul. At this point, Lewis would have inquired of Wielenberg why he affirms the truth of naturalism, which would likely take us back to matters discussed in Section 1.

---

[220] Wielenberg, *God and the Reach of Reason*, 112.
[221] Wielenberg, *God and the Reach of Reason*, 118.

4.4 The Christian Myth

According to Lewis, 'Christianity is not the conclusion of a philosophical debate on the origins of the universe: it is a catastrophic historical event ... It is not a system into which we have to fit the awkward fact of pain: it is itself one of the awkward facts which have to be fitted into any system we make'.[222] What did Lewis think makes it possible to fit the incarnation, death, and resurrection of Jesus Christ into the theistic system? Three related considerations warrant discussion.

First, Lewis believed we need to recognize an important truth about the nature of pleasure and the attainment of the perfect happiness for which we are created. Concerning pleasure's nature, Lewis maintained that while an experience of pleasure often accompanies an action, it is essentially a passion. That is, a person is passive, a patient, with respect to the experience of pleasure. The philosopher Gerd van Riel captures this point in the following quote concerning listening to Beethoven's fourth piano concerto:

> [W]e never know for sure what to do in order to attain pleasure: it is never guaranteed. As an additional element, pleasure can occur, but it is just as likely to fail to appear. [Consider] Beethoven's fourth piano concerto. It is not certain that I will experience pleasure in attending a performance of this work. Even if all the circumstances are in an optimal state, I cannot be sure that I will enjoy the concert... If this is true, it should be possible that an activity is perfectly performed even without yielding pleasure. But this dismisses the immediate link between pleasure and a perfect activity, and moreover, it implies that the perfection of an activity is not enough to secure our pleasure. Even if all circumstances are perfectly arranged, and the activity perfectly performed, pleasure is not guaranteed. This 'escape from our control' is not an accidental quality of pleasure, dependent on circumstances, but a characteristic of the very essence of pleasure.[223]

Because experiences of pleasure compose happiness, an experience of happiness is something over which a person has no absolute control. As van Riel writes, pleasure is like happiness in so far as 'it is something which we may hope to attain, without ever being sure how to behave in order to guarantee its appearance'.[224] In light of the fact that an experience of pleasure is a passion, Lewis concluded that with respect to our own attempts to achieve happiness, our success is a matter of luck: '[A] "right to happiness" ... sounds to me as odd as

---

[222] Lewis, *The Problem of Pain*, 14.
[223] Gerd van Riel, 'Does Perfect Activity Necessarily Yield Pleasure? An Evaluation of the Relation between Pleasure and Activity in Aristotle, Nicomachean Ethics VII and X', *International Journal of Philosophical Studies* 7 (1999): 219–20.
[224] Van Riel, 'Does Perfect Activity Necessarily Yield Pleasure?', 219.

a right to good luck. For I believe ... that we depend for a very great deal of our happiness ... on circumstances outside all human control'.[225] Indeed, in agreement with other hedonists about happiness, Lewis believed that matters concerning our achievement of happiness through our own efforts have a paradoxical character about them. All too often, the more one makes the attainment of happiness the object of one's activity, the more elusive the attainment of it becomes. John Stuart Mill, a hedonist about happiness, wrote the following in his autobiography: 'I now thought that this end [happiness] was only to be attained by not making it the direct end. Those only are happy (I thought) who have their minds fixed on some object other than their own happiness... Aiming thus at something else, they find happiness by the way'.[226] And the philosopher Henry Sidgwick, following Mill, acknowledged as the 'fundamental paradox of Hedonism, that the impulse towards pleasure, if too predominant, defeats its own aim'.[227] In letters to two readers of his books, Lewis wrote the following about happiness and pleasure: 'How right you are: the great thing is to stop thinking about happiness. Indeed the best thing about happiness itself is that it liberates you from thinking about happiness – as the greatest pleasure that money can give us is to make it unnecessary to think about money'.[228] And, 'there is no use trying to keep the first thrill. It will come to life again and again only on *one* condition: that we turn our backs on it and get to work and go through all the dullness'.[229]

Lewis regarded the paradox of hedonism as an instance of a more general 'curious and unhappy psychological law' that our psychological 'attitudes often inhibit the very thing they are intended to facilitate... [For example], a couple never felt less in love than on their wedding day, many a man never felt less merry than at Christmas dinner, and when at a lecture we say "I *must* attend", attention instantly vanishes'.[230] And again, '[t]he dutiful effort prevents the spontaneous feeling; just as if you say to an old friend during a brief reunion "Now let's have a good talk" both suddenly find themselves with nothing to say'.[231] 'Even in social life, you will never make a good impression on other people until you stop thinking about what sort of impression you are making'.[232]

Second, if perfect happiness is the purpose for which we are created and we cannot achieve it on our own terms (the attempt to do so, Lewis believed, is the

---

[225] Lewis, 'We Have No Right to Happiness', 318.
[226] John Stuart Mill, *The Autobiography of John Stuart Mill* (Signet Classics, 1964), 112.
[227] Henry Sidgwick, *The Methods of Ethics*, 7th ed. (Dover, 1966), 48.
[228] Lewis, *The Collected Letters, Volume III*, 93.
[229] Lewis, *The Collected Letters, Volume III*, 698.
[230] Lewis, *The Collected Letters: Volume III*, 1023.
[231] Lewis, *The Collected Letters, Volume III*, 1075.   [232] Lewis, *Mere Christianity*, 226.

essence of immorality) and through our own efforts, how can it be had? Lewis answered, through death to self. He believed that just as we must acknowledge that our existence is a gift, so also we must abandon our efforts to achieve perfect happiness on our own terms and instead receive it as a gift. Lewis wrote that when God makes clear that human beings must lose 'their selves, He means only abandoning the clamour of self-will'.[233] Death to self is a choice 'to bring your picture of yourself down to something nearer life-size'.[234] '[W]e have got to *die*'.[235] Lewis remembered that for him learning to dive into water had 'important (religious) connections'[236] in terms of death to self. In *The Pilgrim's Regress*, the main character John says "'Alas ... I have never learned to dive." "There is nothing to learn," said she [Mother Kirk, who represented the Christian church]. "The art of diving is not to do anything new but simply to cease doing something. You have only to let yourself go"'.[237] '[T]hat is an old paradox; "he that loseth his life shall save it"'.[238] 'This is the ultimate law – the seed dies to live'.[239] The perfect happiness of 'eternal life ... will be eternal dying'.[240]

Lewis emphasized that the idea of death to self is not a Christian idea in the sense that it is found only within the Christian faith. Lewis turned to examples found in nature, mystery religions, Buddhism, and elsewhere to make his point:

> The doctrine of death which I describe is not peculiar to Christianity. Nature herself has written it large across the world in the repeated drama of the buried seed and the re-arising corn. From nature, perhaps, the oldest agricultural communities learned it and with animal, or human, sacrifices showed forth for centuries the truth that 'without shedding of blood is no remission'; and though at first such conceptions may have concerned only the crops and offspring of the tribe, they came later, in the Mysteries, to concern the spiritual death and resurrection of the individual. The Indian ascetic, mortifying his body on a bed of spikes, preaches the same lesson; the Greek philosopher tells us that the life of wisdom is 'a practice of death'. The sensitive and noble heathen of modern times makes his imagined gods 'die into life'. Mr Huxley expounds 'non-attachment'. We cannot escape the doctrine by ceasing to be Christians. It is an 'eternal gospel' revealed to men wherever men have sought, or endured, the truth: it is the very nerve of redemption, which anatomizing wisdom at all times and in all places lays bare ... The peculiarity of the Christian faith is not to teach this doctrine but to render it, in various ways, more tolerable. Christianity teaches us that the

---

[233] Lewis, *The Screwtape Letters and Screwtape Proposes a Toast*, 59.
[234] C. S. Lewis, 'The Seeing Eye', in *Christian Reflections*, ed. Walter Hooper (Eerdmans, [1963] in 1967), 169.
[235] Lewis, *The Collected Letters, Volume I*, 926.
[236] Lewis, *The Collected Letters, Volume I*, 915.   [237] Lewis, *The Pilgrim's Regress*, 166–7.
[238] Lewis, *An Experiment in Criticism*, 138.   [239] Lewis, *The Problem of Pain*, 154.
[240] Lewis, *The Problem of Pain*, 157.

terrible task has already in some sense been accomplished for us – that a master's hand is holding ours as we attempt to trace the difficult letters and that our script need only be a 'copy', not an original. Again, where other systems expose our total nature to death (as in Buddhist renunciation) Christianity demands only that we set right a *misdirection* in our nature, and has no quarrel, like Plato, with the body as such, nor with the psychical elements in our make-up.[241]

In Christianity, death to self does not mean, as it does mean in the Buddhist understanding of the idea, the denial of the existence of the self as an entity that subsists through time. In a letter to his friend Leo Baker in July, 1921, Lewis shared his thoughts about a book, provided to him by Baker, on Buddhism entitled *The Gospel of Buddha According to Old Records*:

[T]hanks for the Gospel of Buddha: in so far as it is a gospel, an exposition of ethics etc, it has not perhaps added much to what I know of the subject, tho' it has been very pleasant reading. On the metaphysical presuppositions of Buddhism, it has given me new light: I did not realize, before, his denial of the Atman [soul or self]: that is very interesting. I cannot at present believe it – to me the Self, as really existing, seems involved in everything we think. No use to talk of 'a bundle of thoughts' etc for, as you know, I always have to ask 'who thinks?' Indeed Buddhism itself does not seem to make much use of the non-Atman doctrine, once it has been stated: and it is only by torture that the theory of re-birth is made compatible with it. Perhaps he has confused a moral truth with a metaphysical fallacy? One sees, of course, its inferiority to Christianity – at any rate as a creed for ordinary men: and though I sometimes feel that complete abnegation is the only real refuge, in my healthier moments I hope that there is something better. This minute I can pine for Nirvana [nothingness], but when the sky clears I shall prefer something with more positive joy.[242]

In sum, Lewis believed that the death and resurrection of Christ 'fit' with already known truths about the nature of pleasure as a passion and the need to die to self to attain the perfect happiness for which we are created. Moreover, he stressed that he would be suspicious of Christianity if it did not share universal truths teased out, even if in misguided ways, in other religions.

[Questioner]: Are not practices like ... self-denial borrowed from earlier or more primitive religions?
   Lewis: I can't say for certain which bits came into Christianity from earlier religions. An enormous amount did. I should find it hard to believe Christianity if that were not so. I couldn't believe that nine-hundred and ninety-nine religions were completely false and the remaining one true.[243]

---

[241] Lewis, *The Problem of Pain*, 102–4.   [242] Lewis, *The Collected Letters, Volume I*, 567.
[243] C. S. Lewis, 'Answers to Questions on Christianity', in *God in the Dock*, ed. Walter Hooper (Eerdmans, [1944] in 1970), 54.

Third, of great importance for Lewis was the mythical nature of non-Christian religions, where a myth is 'an account of what *may have been* the historical fact',[244] a story that is 'fantastic [and] deals with impossibles and preternaturals [and from which we have an] experience [that is] awe-inspiring. We feel it to be numinous'.[245] It 'points ... to the realm [that the reader] lives in most [and] is a master key'[246] whose narrative nature opens up our intellectual vision to see how to connect facts together in a way that makes best sense of things. 'The value of myth is that it takes all the things we know [e.g., the soul, pleasure, the paradoxes of hedonism and losing one's life to save it] and restores to them the rich significance which has been hidden by "the veil of familiarity"'.[247] In light of the first two considerations of this section, it is not surprising that Lewis regarded the idea of a dying-and-rising god as a powerful myth. As a boy, Lewis had read about the Norse god Balder and was struck by the following words from a poem by Henry Wadsworth Longfellow entitled *Tegner's Drapa*:

> *I heard a voice that cried,*
> *Balder the beautiful*
> *Is dead, is dead –* [248]

Balder was mythical. So also, thought Lewis, was Christ. But one thing that distinguished Christ from Balder is that Christ was God in a *true* myth:

> The heart of Christianity is a myth which is also a fact. The old myth of the Dying God, *without ceasing to be myth*, comes down from the heaven of legend and imagination to the earth of history. It *happens* – at a particular date, in a particular place, followed by definable historical consequences. We pass from a Balder or an Osiris, dying nobody knows when or where, to a historical Person crucified ... *under Pontius Pilate*. By becoming fact it does not cease to be myth ... To be truly Christian we must both assent to the historical fact and also receive the myth (fact though it has become) with the same imaginative embrace which we accord to all myths.[249]
>
> My present view ... would be that ... the truth first appears in *mythical* form and then by a long process of condensing or focusing finally becomes incarnate as History... Myth in general is ... a real though unfocused gleam of divine truth falling on human imagination. The Hebrews, like other people,

---

[244] Lewis, *The Problem of Pain*, 71, footnote 3.   [245] Lewis, *An Experiment in Criticism*, 44.
[246] C. S. Lewis, 'Tolkien's The Lord of the Rings', in *On Stories and Other Essays on Literature*, ed. Walter Hooper (Harcourt Brace, [1954 and 1955] in 1982), 85.
[247] Lewis, 'Tolkien's The Lord of the Rings', 90. Lewis believed that a myth, because it is a story with a narrative, must have things about which to narrate. He assumed that two essential things about which the Christian myth narrates are the soul and the purpose for which it is created, which is the experience of pleasure (happiness).
[248] Lewis, *Surprised by Joy*, 17.
[249] C. S. Lewis, 'Myth Became Fact', in *God in the Dock*, ed. Walter Hooper (Eerdmans, [1944] in 1970), 66–7.

had mythology: but as they were the chosen people so their mythology was the chosen mythology – the mythology chosen by God to be the vehicle of the earliest sacred truths, the first step in that process which ends in the New Testament where truth has become completely historical.[250]

Lewis wrote, 'I have been reading ... legends [and] myths all my life. I know what they are like'.[251] He was convinced he knew the distinction between a false and a true myth, as did an atheist philosophy colleague T. D. Weldon:

> The real clue had been put into my hand by that hard-boiled Atheist [Weldon] when he said, 'Rum thing, all that about the Dying God. Seems to have really happened once'; by him and by Barfield's encouragement of a more respectful, if not more delighted, attitude to Pagan myth. The question was no longer to find the one simply true religion among a thousand religions simply false. It was rather, 'Where has religion reached its true maturity? Where, if anywhere, have the hints of all Paganism been fulfilled?'[252]

Lewis concluded that the hints of all paganism had been fulfilled in Christ. The myth of God's descent, death, and resurrection in Christ made sense in light of other things we already know, not only pagan myths but also, and most importantly, the 'universal principle'[253] that we must die to self in order to rise to experience the perfect happiness for which we are created.

Lewis believed that another part of the interpretive backdrop to the incarnation and rising of God, of descent and ascent, was provided by our knowledge of the soul-body distinction. In answer to the question 'What can be meant by "God becoming man"? In what sense is it conceivable that eternal self-existent Spirit ... should be so combined with a natural human organism as to make one person?',[254] Lewis answered that we understand the incarnation because we have an awareness of the soul-body distinction in our own embodiment so that

> the difficulty which we felt in the mere idea of the Supernatural descending into the Natural is apparently non-existent, or is at least overcome in the person of every man. If we did not know by experience what it feels like to be a rational animal ... we could not conceive, much less imagine, the [Incarnation] happening. The discrepancy between a movement of atoms in an astronomer's cortex and his understanding that there must be a still unobserved planet beyond Uranus, is already so immense that the Incarnation of God Himself is, in one sense, scarcely more startling.[255]

---

[250] Lewis, *Miracles*, 218, footnote 1.
[251] C. S. Lewis, 'Modern Theology and Biblical Criticism', in *Christian Reflections*, ed. Walter Hooper (Eerdmans, [1959] in 1967), 155.
[252] Lewis, *Surprised by Joy*, 235. [253] Lewis, 'Myth Became Fact', 66.
[254] Lewis, *Miracles*, 176. [255] Lewis, *Miracles*, 177–8.

Not only soul-body dualism illuminates the incarnation, death, and resurrection motif. Different aspects of nature also provide a similar illumination of the idea of descent and ascent:

> In this descent and reascent everyone will recognize a familiar pattern: a thing written all over the world. It is the pattern of all vegetable life. It must belittle itself into something hard, small and deathlike, it must fall into the ground: thence the new life reascends. It is the pattern of all animal generation too. There is descent from the full and perfect organisms into the spermatozoon and ovum, and in the dark womb a life at first inferior in kind to that of the species which is being reproduced: then the slow ascent to the perfect embryo, to the living, conscious baby, and finally to the adult.[256]

However, Lewis thought that the pattern of descent and ascent in nature is once again illuminated by what is known about ourselves. Lewis completed the thoughts just quoted with the following words: '[so the descent and reascent pattern in nature] is also in our moral and emotional life. The first innocent and spontaneous desires have to submit to the deathlike process of control and total denial'.[257]

4.5 Chronological Snobbery

While in his younger years Lewis found the myth of a dying-and-rising god imaginatively pleasing, its origins were ancient and, thereby, rationally suspect to modern thought. However, he recounted that in his twenties his friend Barfield

> destroyed forever two elements in my own thought, [one of which was] my 'chronological snobbery', [my] uncritical acceptance of the intellectual climate common to our own age and the assumption that whatever has gone out of date is on that account discredited. [Barfield made clear to me that you] must find why it went out of date. Was it ever refuted (and if so by whom, where, and how conclusively) or did it merely die away as fashions do? If the latter, this tells us nothing about its truth or falsehood. From seeing this, one passes to the realization that our own age is also 'a period', and certainly has, like all periods, its own characteristic illusions. They are likeliest to lurk in

---

[256] Lewis, *Miracles*, 180.
[257] Lewis, *Miracles*, 180. Lewis wrote, 'I believe in Christianity as I believe that the Sun has risen, not only because I see it, but because by it I see everything else' (C. S. Lewis, 'Is Theology Poetry?', in *The Weight of Glory and Other Addresses*, ed. Walter Hooper (Eerdmans, [1944] in 2011), 140). He did not mean that except for the sun itself he did not know anything else without his belief in Christianity. Rather, as he wrote immediately before the sentence just quoted, he believed that 'Christian theology [the Christian myth] can fit in science, art, morality, and the sub-Christian religions' (Lewis, 'Is Theology Poetry?', 140), each of which is known independently of a belief in Christianity.

those widespread assumptions which are so ingrained in the age that no one dares to attack or feels it necessary to defend them.[258]

Our intellectual climate is naturalism. 'We all', wrote Lewis, 'have Naturalism in our bones',[259] and we take for granted what follows from it: the exclusion of reason and the existence of the soul; the elimination of the intrinsic goodness of pleasure and the perfect happiness of the afterlife; and the denial of the existence of God. Because Lewis dared to attack naturalism, he was intellectually able to affirm the integrity of our reasoning, the soul's existence, the intrinsic goodness of pleasure and the fulfilment of our desire for perfect happiness, and God's existence. Finally, he recognized in the person of Jesus of Nazareth the truth of the dying-and-rising-god myth that he found imaginatively pleasing. In words Lewis wrote and were quoted in the Introduction, 'I was brought back [to Christianity] ... [b]y Philosophy'.

---

[258] Lewis, *Surprised by Joy*, 207–8.   [259] Lewis, *Miracles*, 268.

Bibliography

Annas, Julia. *The Morality of Happiness*. Oxford University Press, 1993.

Anscombe, Elizabeth. 'A Reply to Mr. C. S. Lewis's Argument that "Naturalism" Is Self-Refuting'. In *The Collected Philosophical Papers of G. E. M. Anscombe: Volume 2, Metaphysics and the Philosophy of Mind*. University of Minnesota Press, [circa 1947] in 1981, 224–32.

Anselm, St. *Anselm of Canterbury: The Major Works*, edited by Brian Davies and G. R. Evans. Oxford University Press, 1998.

Aquinas, St. Thomas. *Summa Contra Gentiles: Book Three*, translated by Vernon J. Bourke. University of Notre Dame Press, 1975.

Augustine, St. 'The Happy Life'. In *Happiness: Classic and Contemporary Readings*, edited by Steven M. Cahn and Christine Vitrano. Oxford University Press, 2008, 51–60.

Baier, Kurt. 'The Meaning of Life'. In *The Meaning of Life*. 2nd ed., edited by E. D. Klemke. Oxford University Press, 2000, 101–32.

Barkman, Adam. *C. S. Lewis & Philosophy as a Way of Life*. Zossima Press, 2009.

Bering, Jesse. 'The Folk Psychology of Souls'. *Behavioral and Brain Sciences* 29 (2006): 453–62.

Beversluis, John. *C. S. Lewis and the Search for Rational Religion*. Eerdmans, 1985.

Bloom, Paul. 'Religion Is Natural'. *Developmental Science* 10 (2007): 147–51.

Boethius. *The Consolation of Philosophy*, translated by S. J. Tester. Harvard University Press, 1973.

Calvin, John. *The Institutes of the Christian Religion*, translated by Henry Beveridge. Hendrickson, 2008.

Carpenter, Humphrey. *J. R. R. Tolkien: A Biography*. Houghton Mifflin, 2000.

Dawkins, Richard. *The Blind Watchmaker*. Norton, 1987.

Dyer, Justin Buckley and Micah Watson. *C. S. Lewis on Politics and the Natural Law*. Cambridge University Press, 2016.

Goetz, Stewart. *A Philosophical Walking Tour with C. S. Lewis: Why It Did Not Include Rome*. Bloomsbury, 2015.

Goetz, Stewart. *C. S. Lewis*. Wiley-Blackwell, 2018.

Goetz, Stewart and Charles Taliaferro. *Naturalism*. Eerdmans, 2008.

Goetz, Stewart and Charles Taliaferro. *A Brief History of the Soul*. Wiley-Blackwell, 2011.

Humphrey, Nicholas. *Soul Dust*. Princeton University Press, 2011.

Kilby, Clyde S. and Marjorie Mead, eds. *Brothers and Friends: The Diaries of Major Warren Hamilton Lewis*. Harper and Row, 1982.

Kim, Jaegwon. *Physicalism, or Something Near Enough*. Princeton University Press, 2005.

Lewis, C. S. *A Preface to Paradise Lost*. Oxford University Press, 1942.

Lewis, C. S. *Surprised by Joy: The Shape of My Early Life*. Harcourt, 1955.

Lewis, C. S. *Reflections on the Psalms*. Harcourt, 1958.

Lewis, C. S. *An Experiment in Criticism*. Cambridge University Press, 1961.

Lewis, C. S. *The Screwtape Letters and Screwtape Proposes a Toast*. Macmillan, 1961.

Lewis, C. S. *The Discarded Image: An Introduction to Medieval and Renaissance Literature*. Cambridge University Press, 1964.

Lewis, C. S. 'Christianity and Culture'. In *Christian Reflections*, edited by Walter Hooper. Eerdmans, 1967, 12–36.

Lewis, C. S. 'De Futilitate'. In *Christian Reflections*, edited by Walter Hooper. Eerdmans, 1967, 57–71.

Lewis, C. S. 'Modern Theology and Biblical Criticism'. In *Christian Reflections*, edited by Walter Hooper. Eerdmans, [1959] in 1967, 152–66.

Lewis, C. S. 'A Note on Jane Austen'. In *Selected Literary Essays*, edited by Walter Hooper. Cambridge University Press, [1954] in 1969, 175–86.

Lewis, C. S. 'Answers to Questions on Christianity'. In *God in the Dock*, edited by Walter Hooper. Eerdmans, [1944] in 1970, 48–62.

Lewis, C. S. 'Bulverism'. In *God in the Dock*, edited by Walter Hooper. Eerdmans, [1944] in 1970, 271–7.

Lewis, C. S. 'Dogma and the Universe'. In *God in the Dock*, edited by Walter Hooper. Eerdmans, [1943] in 1970, 38–47.

Lewis, C. S. 'Evil and God'. In *God in the Dock*, edited by Walter Hooper. Eerdmans, [1941] in 1970, 21–4.

Lewis, C. S. 'Is Progress Possible?' In *God in the Dock*, edited by Walter Hooper. Eerdmans, [1958] in 1970, 311–16.

Lewis, C. S. 'Is Theism Important?' In *God in the Dock*, edited by Walter Hooper. Eerdmans, [1952] in 1970, 172–6.

Lewis, C. S. 'Man or Rabbit?' In *God in the Dock*, edited by Walter Hooper. Eerdmans, [1946?] in 1970, 108–13.

Lewis, C. S. 'Meditation in a Toolshed'. In *God in the Dock*, edited by Walter Hooper. Eerdmans, [1945] in 1970, 212–15.

Lewis, C. S. 'Myth Became Fact'. In *God in the Dock*, edited by Walter Hooper. Eerdmans, [1944] in 1970, 63–7.

Lewis, C. S. 'Rejoinder to Dr Pittenger'. In *God in the Dock*, edited by Walter Hooper. Harcourt, [1958] in 1970, 177–83.

Lewis, C. S. 'Religion without Dogma?' In *God in the Dock*, edited by Walter Hooper. Eerdmans, [1946] in 1970, 129–46.

Lewis, C. S. 'The Pains of Animals'. *In God in the Dock*, edited by Walter Hooper. Eerdmans, [1950] in 1970, 161–71.

Lewis, C. S. 'Two Ways with the Self'. In *God in the Dock*, edited by Walter Hooper. Eerdmans, [1940] in 1970, 193–5.

Lewis, C. S. 'Vivisection'. In *God in the Dock*, edited by Walter Hooper. Eerdmans, [1947] in 1970, 224–8.

Lewis, C. S. 'We Have No Right to Happiness'. In *God in the Dock*, edited by Walter Hooper. Eerdmans, [1963] in 1970, 317–22.

Lewis, C. S. 'What Are We to Make of Jesus Christ?' In *God in the Dock*, edited by Walter Hooper. Eerdmans, [1950] in 1970, 156–60.

Lewis, C. S. 'A Reply to Professor Haldane'. In *On Stories and Other Essays on Literature*, edited by Walter Hooper. Harcourt Brace, [1966] in 1982, 74–85.

Lewis, C. S. 'On Three Ways of Writing for Children'. In *On Stories and Other Essays on Literature*, edited by Walter Hooper. Harcourt Brace, [1952] in 1982, 31–43.

Lewis, C. S. 'Tolkien's *The Lord of the Rings*'. In *On Stories and Other Essays on Literature*, edited by Walter Hooper. Harcourt Brace, [1954 and 1955] in 1982, 83–90.

Lewis, C. S. 'Hedonics'. In *Present Concerns: A Compelling Collection of Timely, Journalistic Essays*, edited by Walter Hooper. Harcourt, [1945] in 1986, 50–5.

Lewis, C. S. 'Modern Man and His Categories of Thought'. In *Present Concerns: A Compelling Collection of Timely, Journalistic Essays*, edited by Walter Hooper. Harcourt, [1946] in 1986, 61–6.

Lewis, C. S. 'On Living in an Atomic Age'. In *Present Concerns: A Compelling Collection of Timely, Journalistic Essays*, edited by Walter Hooper. Harcourt, [1948] in 1986, 73–80.

Lewis, C. S. 'The Empty Universe'. In *Present Concerns: A Compelling Collection of Timely, Journalistic Essays*, edited by Walter Hooper. Harcourt, [1952] in 1986, 81–6.

Lewis, C. S. 'Three Kinds of Men'. In *Present Concerns: A Compelling Collection of Timely, Journalistic Essays*, edited by Walter Hooper. Harcourt, [1943] in 1986, 21–2.

Lewis, C. S. 'On Obstinacy in Belief'. In *The World's Last Night and Other Essays*, edited by Walter Hooper. Harcourt, [1955] in 1987, 13–30.

Lewis, C. S. *The Four Loves*. Harcourt [1960] 1988.

Lewis, C. S. *All My Road before Me: The Diary of C. S. Lewis*, edited by Walter Hooper. Harcourt, 1991.

Lewis, C. S. *Letters to Malcolm: Chiefly on Prayer*. Harcourt, [1964] 1992.
Lewis, C. S. *The Pilgrim's Regress*. Eerdmans, [1933] 1992.
Lewis, C. S. *A Grief Observed*. HarperSanFrancisco, [1961] 2001.
Lewis, C. S. 'Is Theology Poetry?' In *The Weight of Glory and Other Addresses*, edited by Walter Hooper. HarperCollins, [1944] in 2001, 116–40.
Lewis, C. S. *Mere Christianity*. HarperSanFrancisco, [1952] 2001.
Lewis, C. S. *Miracles: A Preliminary Study*. 2nd ed. HarperSanFrancisco, [1960] 2001.
Lewis, C. S. *The Abolition of Man*. HarperSanFrancisco, [1944] 2001.
Lewis, C. S. *The Great Divorce*. HarperSanFrancisco, [1946] 2001.
Lewis, C. S. *The Problem of Pain*. HarperSanFrancisco, [1940] 2001.
Lewis, C. S. 'The Weight of Glory'. In *The Weight of Glory and Other Addresses*, edited by Walter Hooper. HarperCollins, [1941] in 2001, 25–46.
Lewis, C. S. *Perelandra*. Scribners, [1944] 2003.
Lewis, C. S. *The Collected Letters of C. S. Lewis: Volume I; Family Letters, 1905–1931*, edited by Walter Hooper. HarperSanFrancisco, 2004.
Lewis, C. S. *The Collected Letters of C. S. Lewis: Volume II; Books, Broadcasts, and the War, 1931–1949*, edited by Walter Hooper. HarperSanFrancisco, 2004.
Lewis, C. S. *The Collected Letters of C. S. Lewis: Volume III; Narnia, Cambridge, and Joy, 1950–1963*, edited by Walter Hooper. HarperSanFrancisco, 2007.
Mac Cumhaill, Clare and Rachel Wiseman. *Metaphysical Animals: How Four Women Brought Philosophy Back to Life*. Chatto & Windus, 2022.
McGrath, Alister. *The Intellectual World of C. S. Lewis*. Wiley-Blackwell, 2014.
Mill, John Stuart. *The Autobiography of John Stuart Mill*. Signet Classics, 1964.
Mill, John Stuart. 'Utilitarianism'. In *Selected Writings of John Stuart Mill*, edited by Maurice Cowling. Mentor, 1968, 243–304.
Paley, William. 'The Watch and the Watchmaker'. In *Philosophy of Religion: An Anthology*, edited by Louis P. Pojman. Wadsworth, [1802] in 1987, 29–31.
Rey, Georges. *Contemporary Philosophy of Mind*. Blackwell, 1997.
Rorty, Richard. *Philosophy and the Mirror of Nature*. Princeton University Press, 1979.
Rosenberg, Alex. *The Atheist's Guide to Reality: Enjoying Life without Illusions*. W. W. Norton, 2011.
Rosenberg, Alex. 'Why I Am a Naturalist'. *The New York Times*, 17 September 2011. https://archive.nytimes.com/opinionator.blogs.nytimes.com/2011/09/17/why-i-am-a-naturalist/
Russell, Bertrand. 'A Free Man's Worship'. In *The Meaning of Life*. 2nd ed., edited by E. D. Klemke. Oxford University Press, [1957] in 2000, 71–7.
Sidgwick, Henry. *The Methods of Ethics*. 7th ed. Dover, 1966.

Stroud, Barry. 'The Charm of Naturalism'. In *Naturalism in Question*, edited by Mario De Caro and David Macarthur. Harvard University Press, 2004, 21–35.

Taylor, Richard. *Metaphysics*. 4th ed. Prentice-Hall, 1992.

Van Inwagen, Peter. 'C. S. Lewis' Argument against Naturalism'. *Journal of Inklings Studies* 1 (2011): 25–40.

Van Riel, Gerd. 'Does Perfect Activity Necessarily Yield Pleasure? An Evaluation of the Relation between Pleasure and Activity in Aristotle, Nicomachean Ethics VII and X'. *International Journal of Philosophical Studies* 7 (1999): 211–41.

Wielenberg, Erik. *God and the Reach of Reason: C. S. Lewis, David Hume, and Bertrand Russell*. Cambridge University Press, 2008.

Williamson, Timothy. 'What Is Naturalism?' *The New York Times*, 4 September 2011. https://archive.nytimes.com/opinionator.blogs.nytimes.com/2011/09/04/what-is-naturalism/

Wolterstorff, Nicholas. *Justice: Rights and Wrongs*. Princeton University Press, 2008.

Acknowledgements

I thank Patrick Casey, Jon Loose, Timothy Mawson, Charles Taliaferro, and Nicholas Waghorn for providing me with comments on various drafts of the manuscript.

To Daniel,
May the childhood pleasure of imitating William be the seed
of the adult pleasure of imitating God.

Cambridge Elements⁼

History of Philosophy and Theology in the West

Alexander J. B. Hampton

University of Toronto

Alexander J. B. Hampton is a professor at the University of Toronto, specialising in metaphysics, poetics, and nature. His publications include *Romanticism and the Re-Invention of Modern Religion* (Cambridge 2019), *Christian Platonism: A History* (ed.) (Cambridge, 2021), and the *Cambridge Companion to Christianity and the Environment* (ed.) (Cambridge, 2022).

Editorial Board

Shaun Blanchard, *University of Notre Dame, Australia*
Jennifer Newsome Martin, *University of Notre Dame, USA*
Sean McGrath, *Memorial University*
Willemien Otten, *University of Chicago*
Catherine Pickstock, *University of Cambridge*
Jacob H. Sherman, *California Institute of Integral Studies*
Charles Taliaferro, *St. Olaf College*

About the Series

In the history of philosophy and theology, many figures and topics are considered in isolation from each other. This series aims to complicate this binary opposition, while covering the history of this complex conversation from antiquity to the present. It reconceptualizes traditional elements of the field, generating new and productive areas of historical enquiry, and advancing creative proposals based upon the recovery of these resources.

Cambridge Elements

History of Philosophy and Theology in the West

Elements in the Series

The Metaphysics of Divine Participation
Alexander J. B. Hampton

C. S. Lewis on the Soul, God, and Christianity
Stewart Goetz

A full series listing is available at: www.cambridge.org/EHPT

For EU product safety concerns, contact us at Calle de José Abascal, 56–1°, 28003 Madrid, Spain or eugpsr@cambridge.org.

www.ingramcontent.com/pod-product-compliance
Ingram Content Group UK Ltd.
Pitfield, Milton Keynes, MK11 3LW, UK
UKHW021634010625
458959UK00020B/585